ACHROMATIC DOMINATION

モノトーンの支配

Yuki Sakurai 櫻井ゆき

Rope and Photographed
by †Siva†

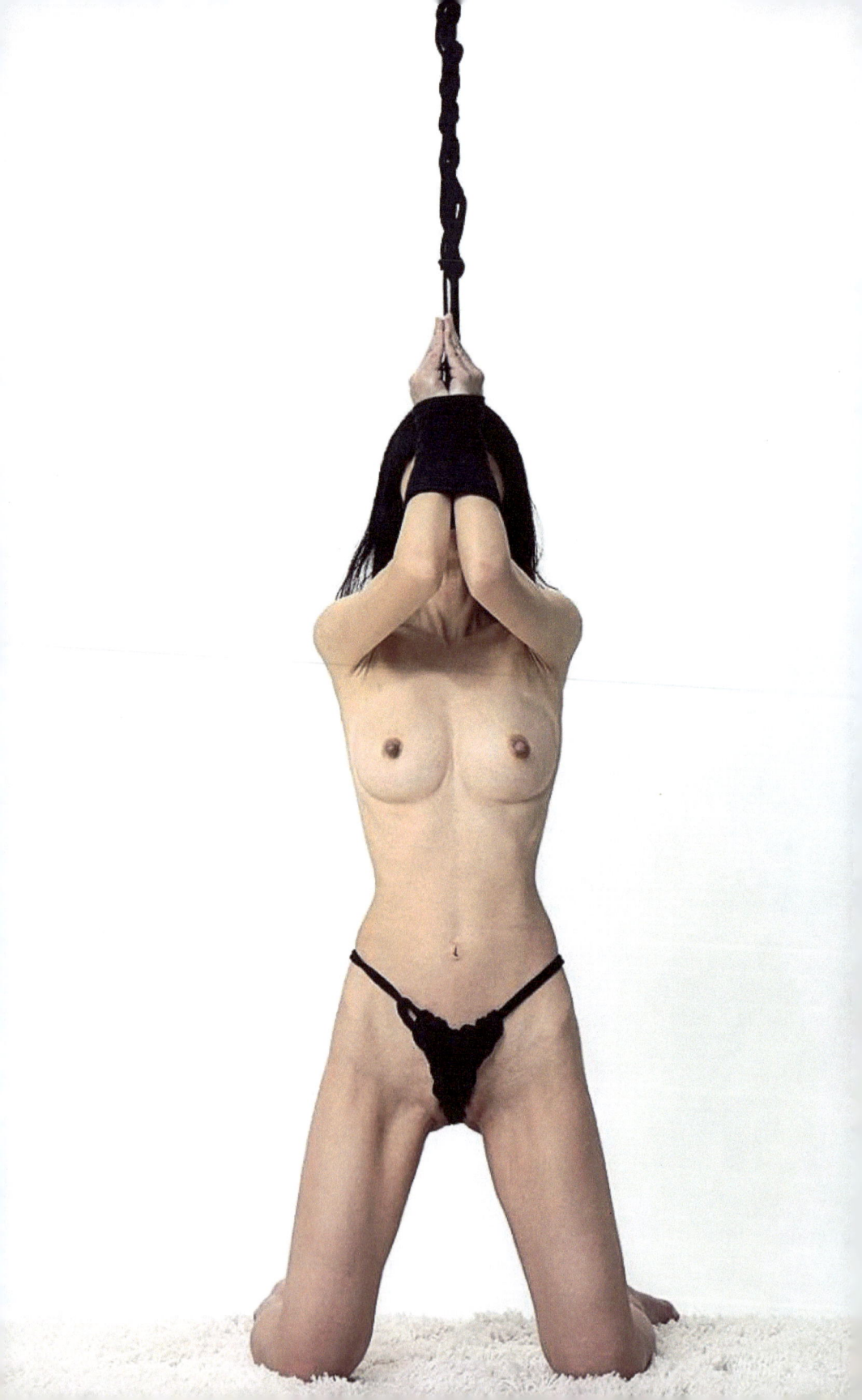

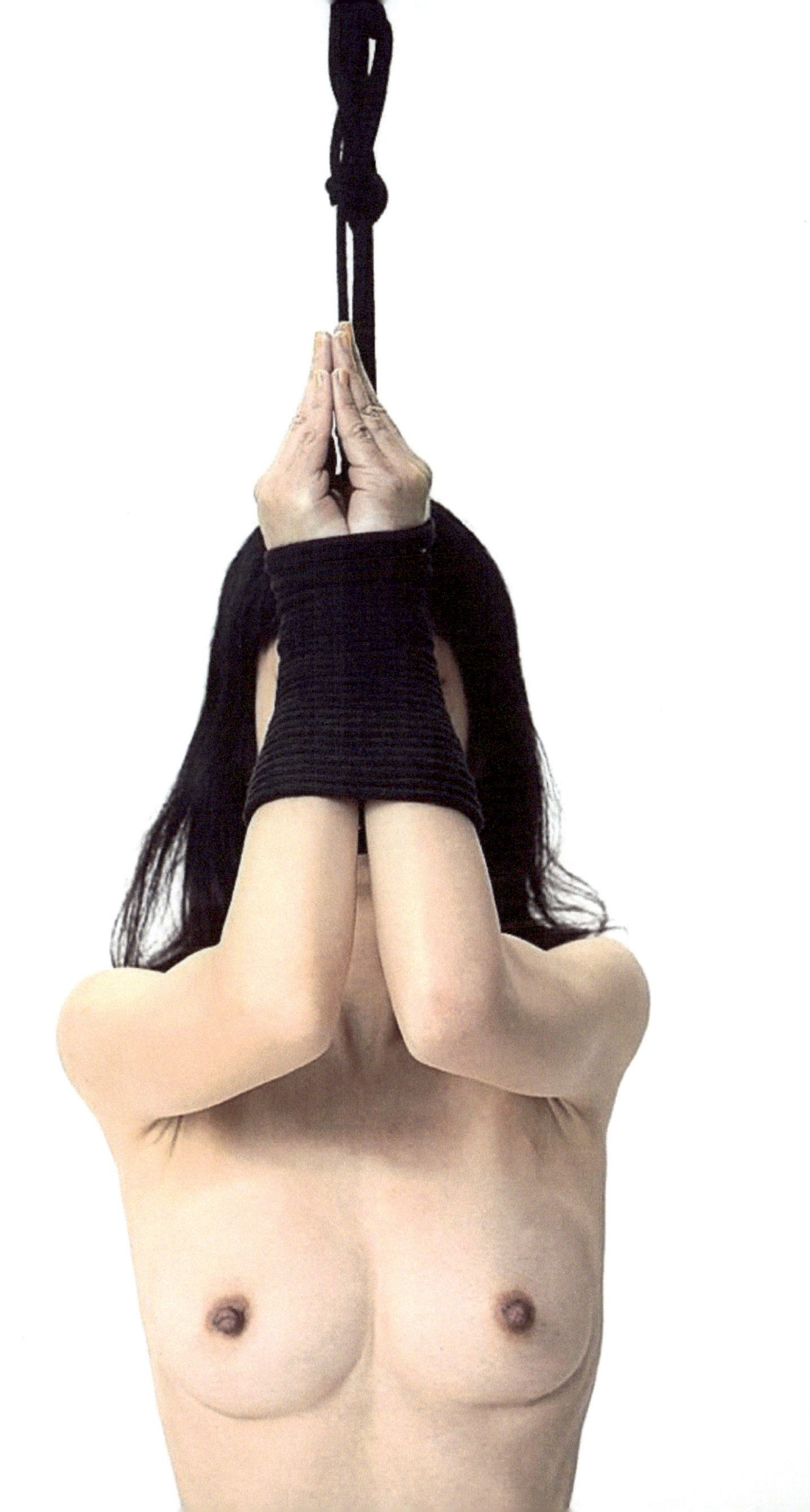

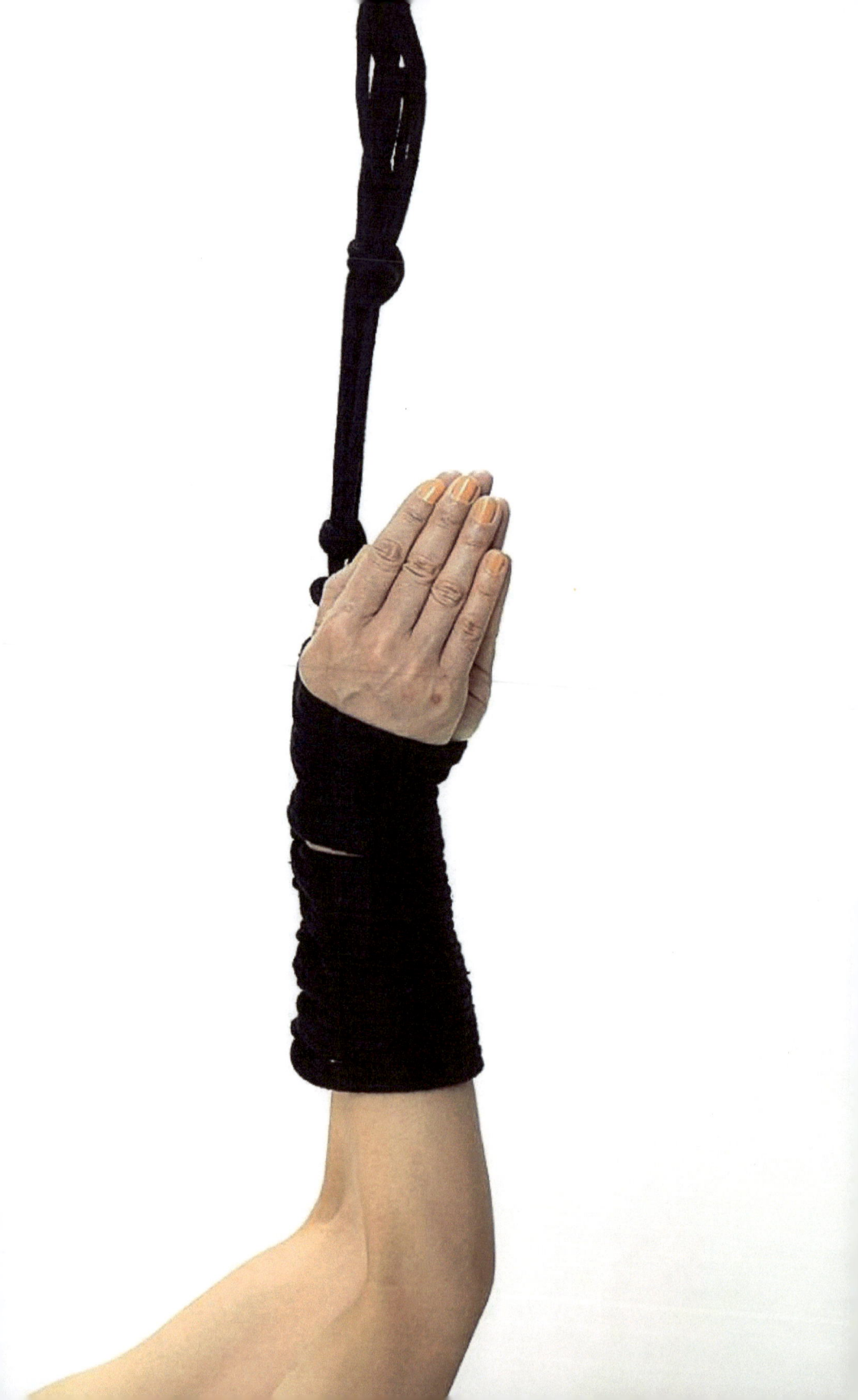

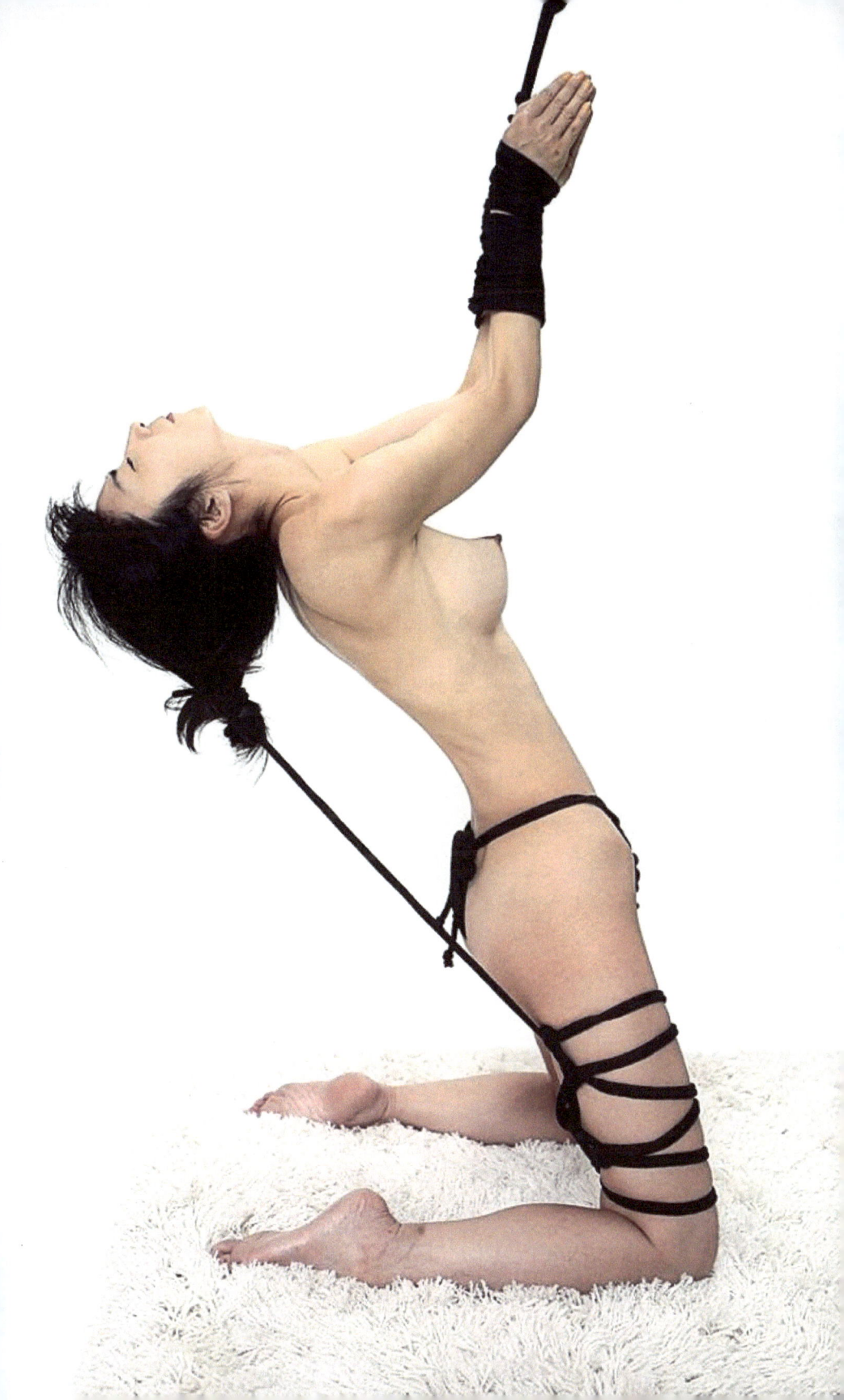

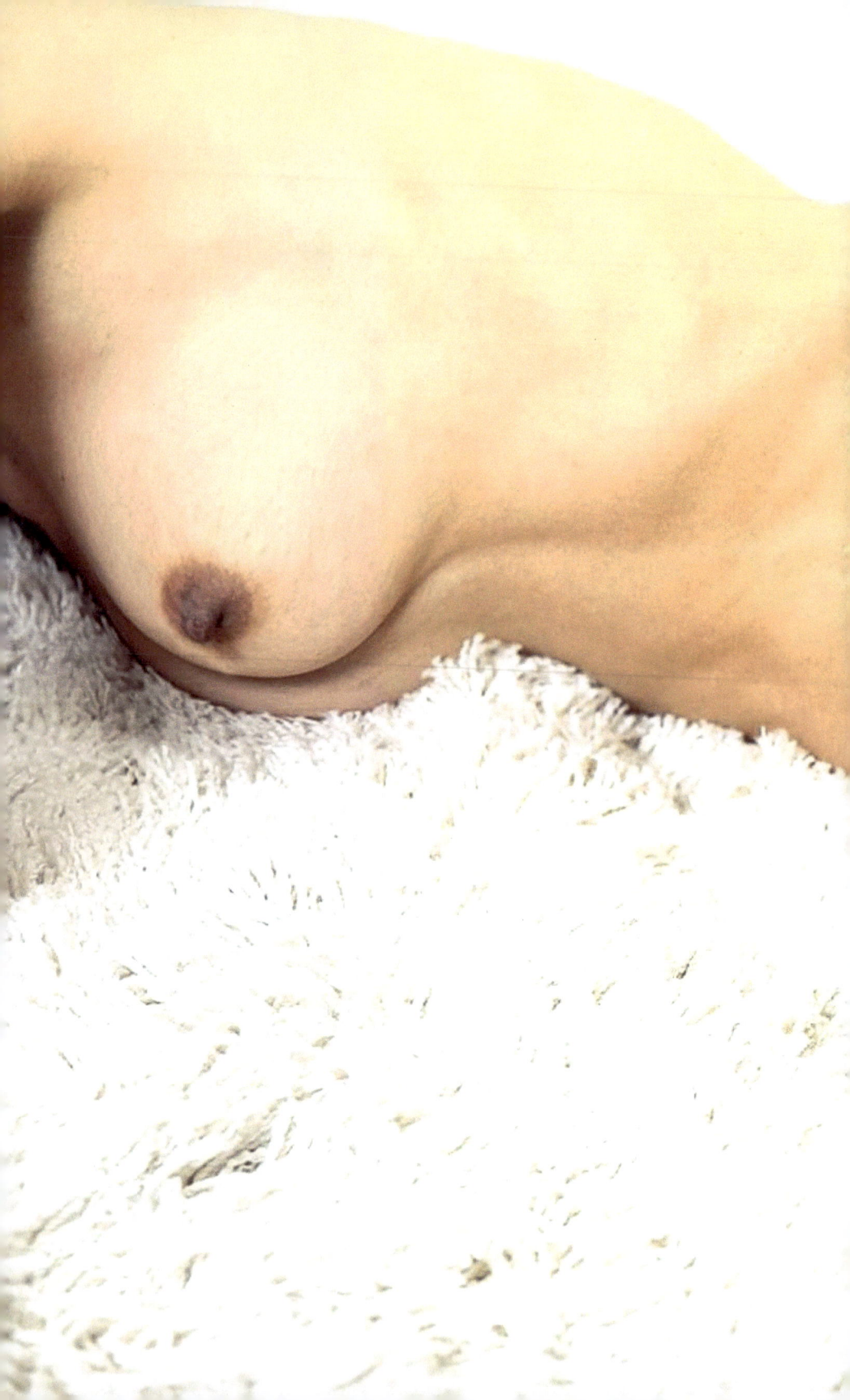

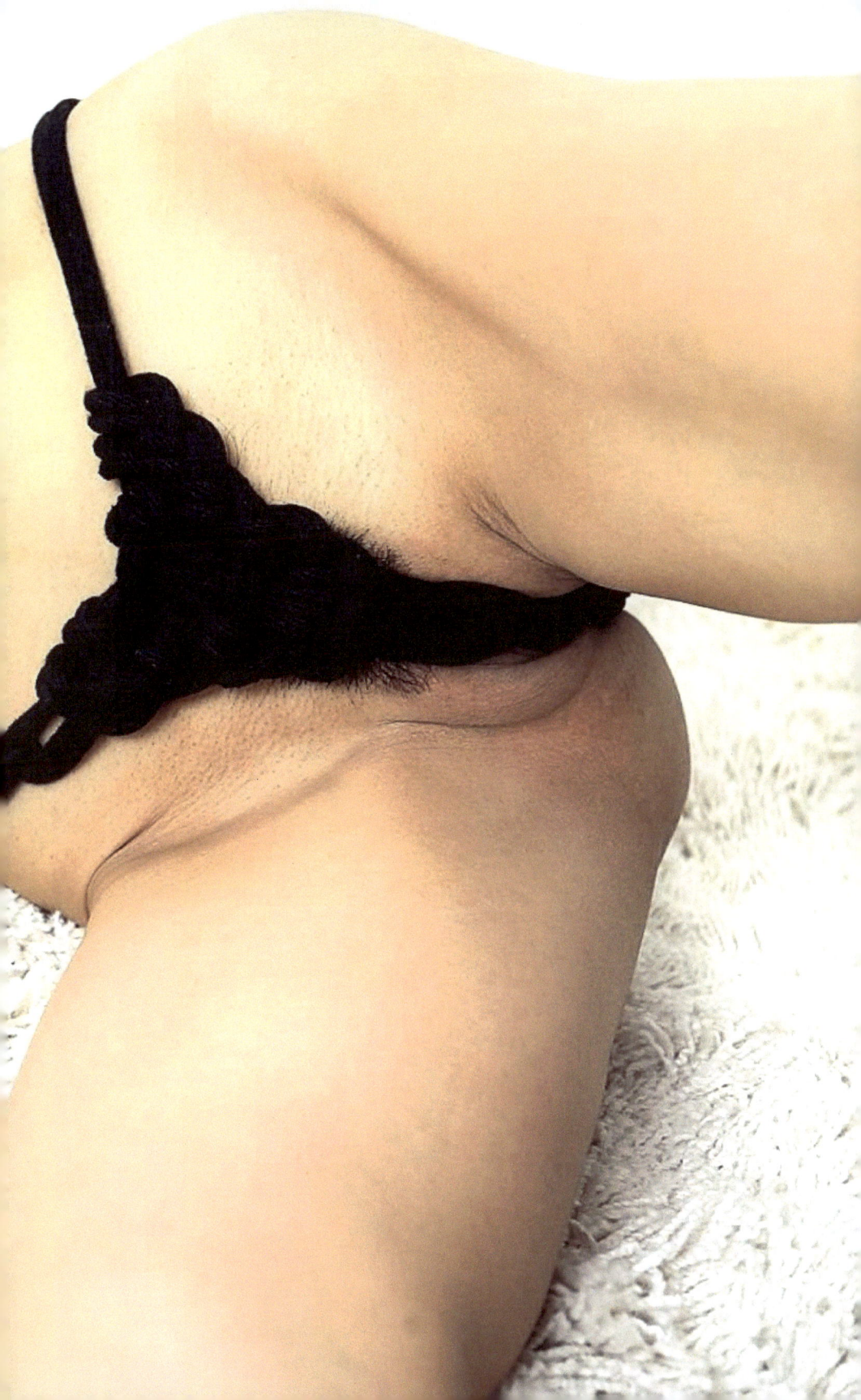

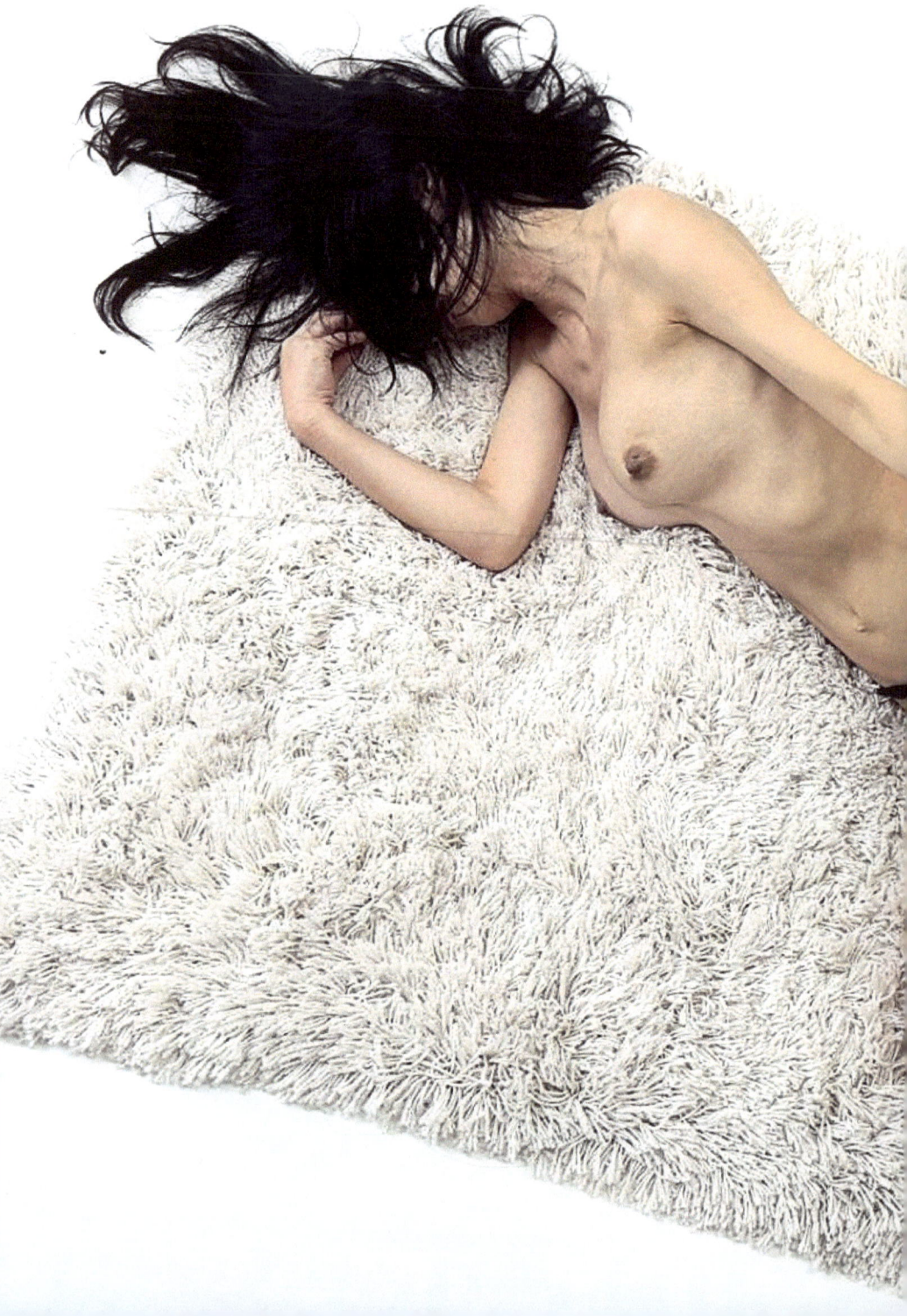

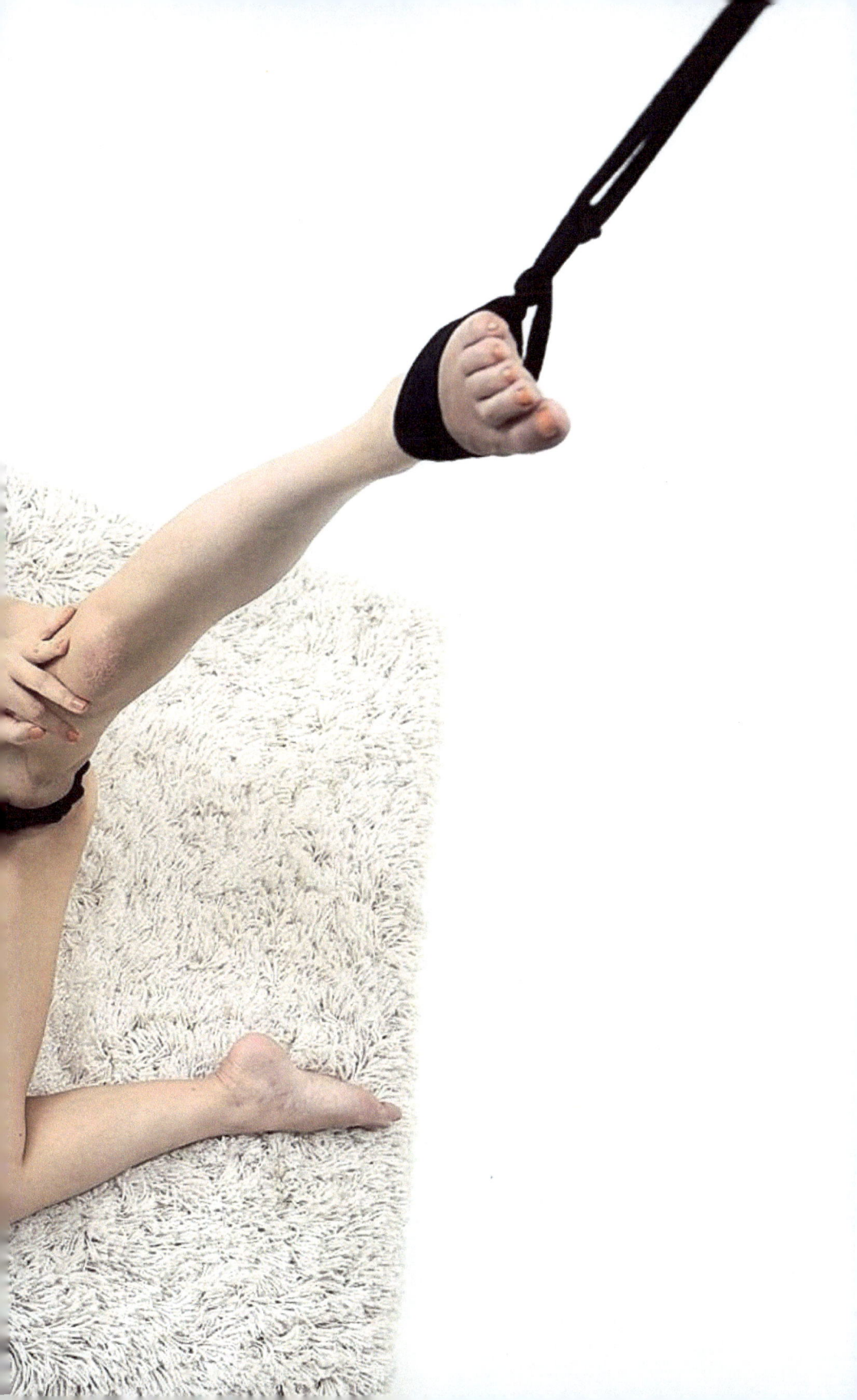

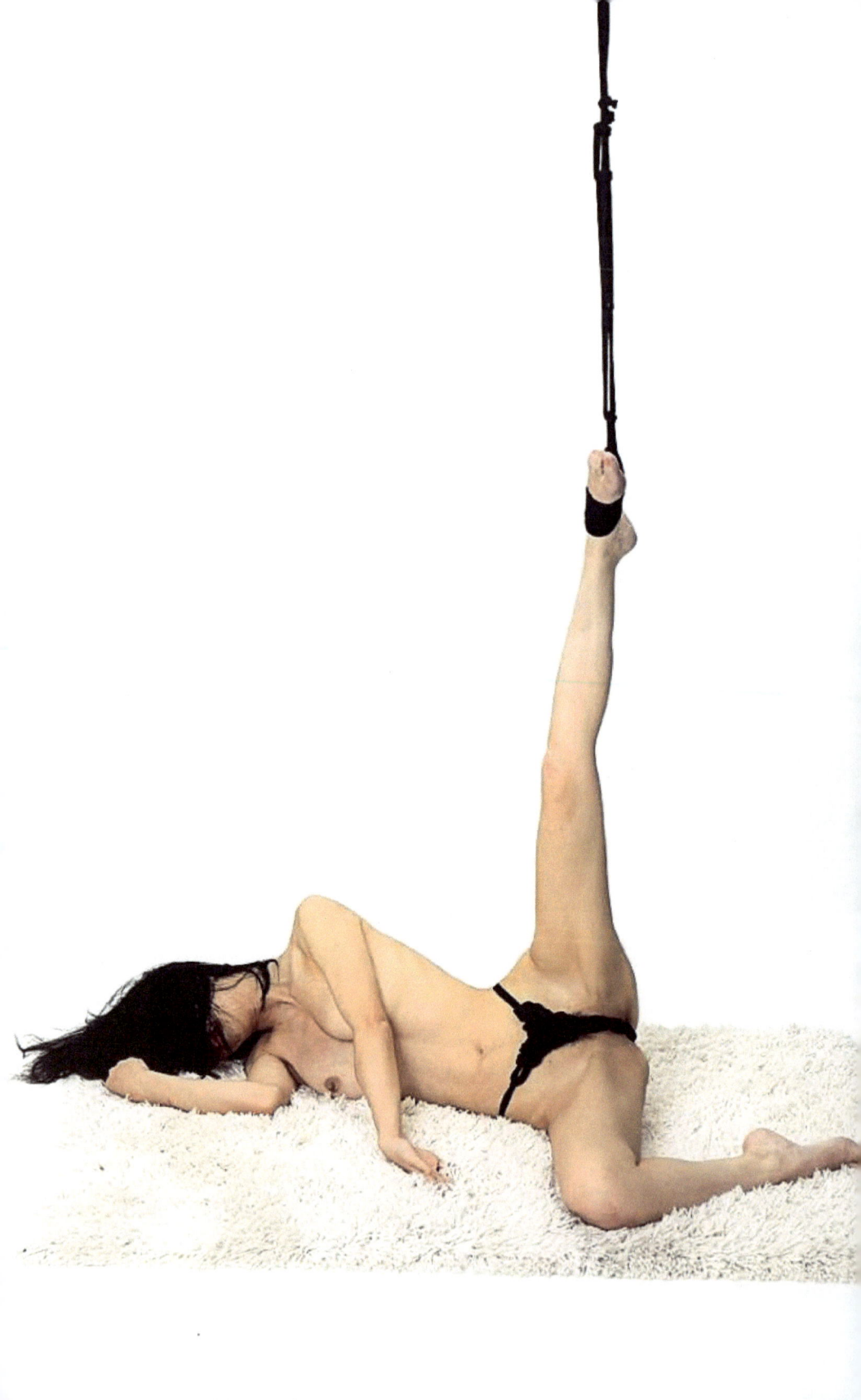

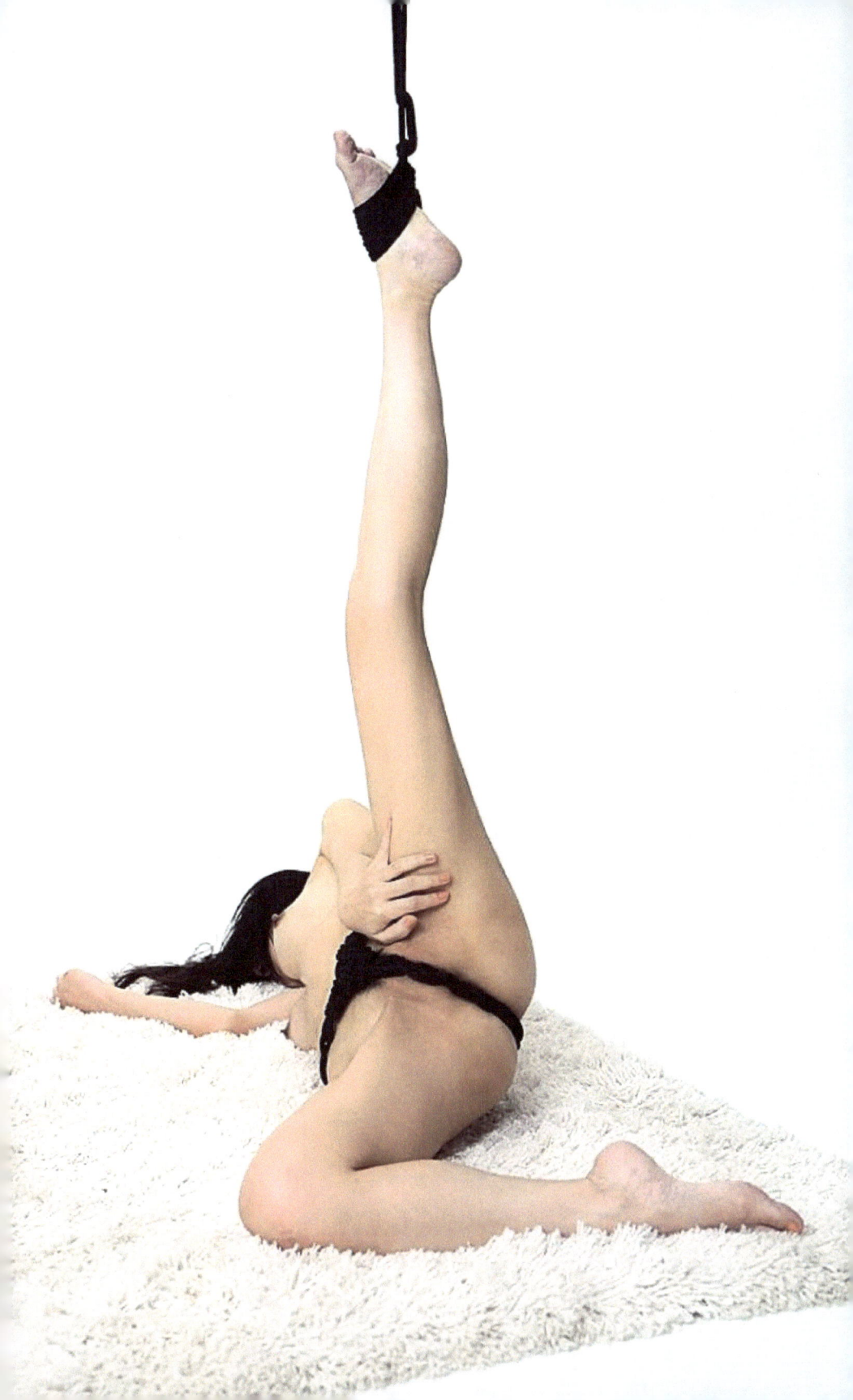

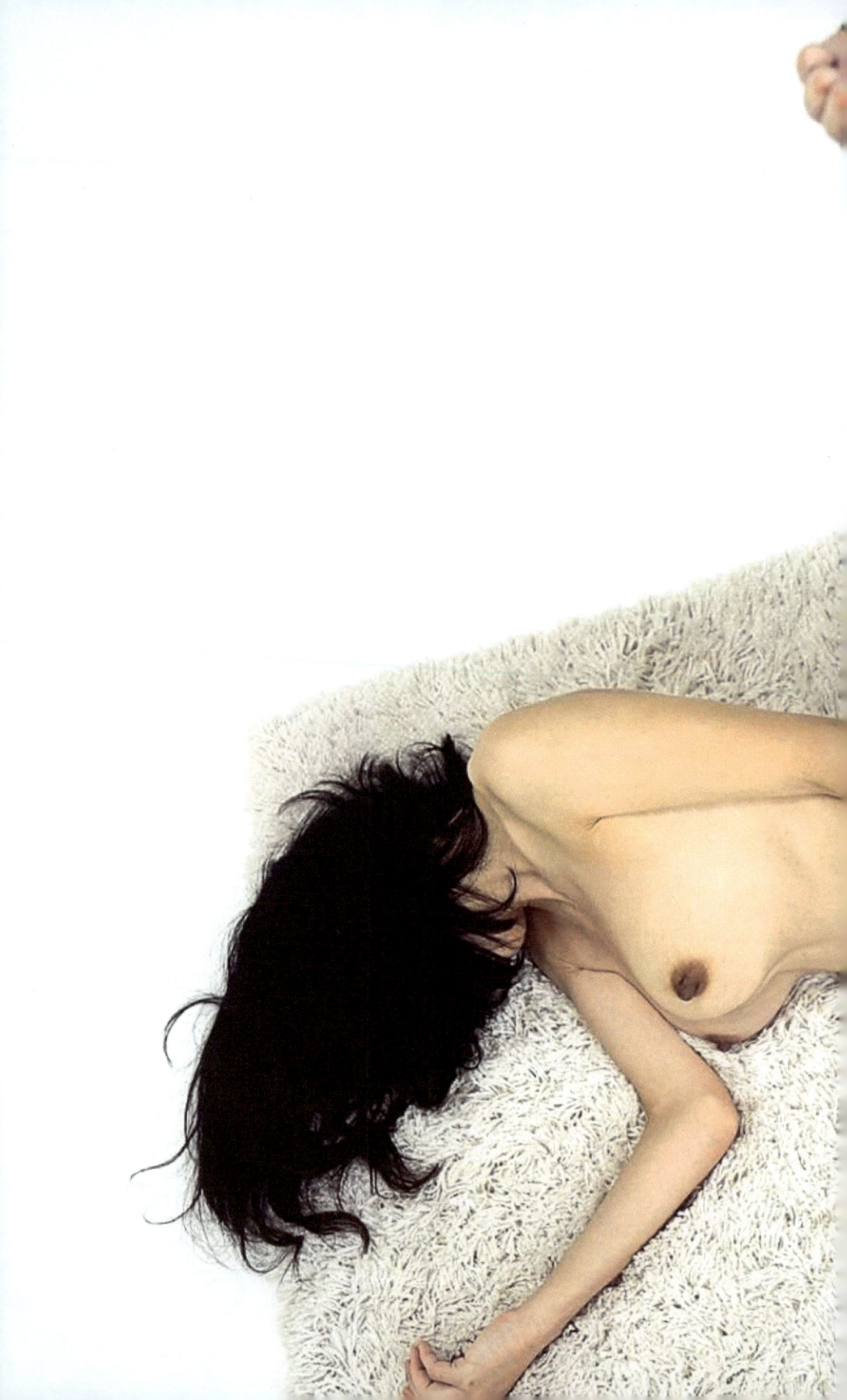

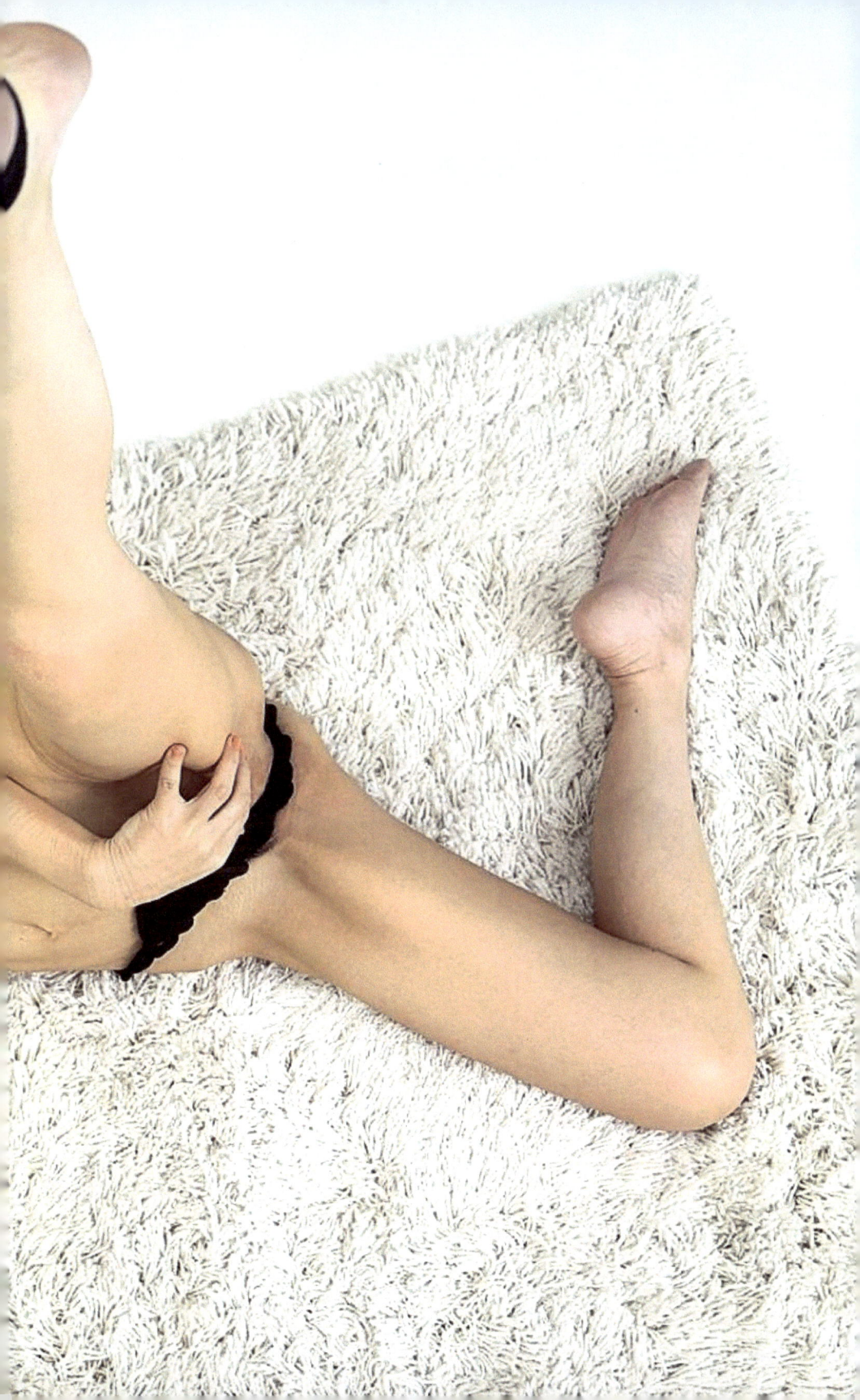

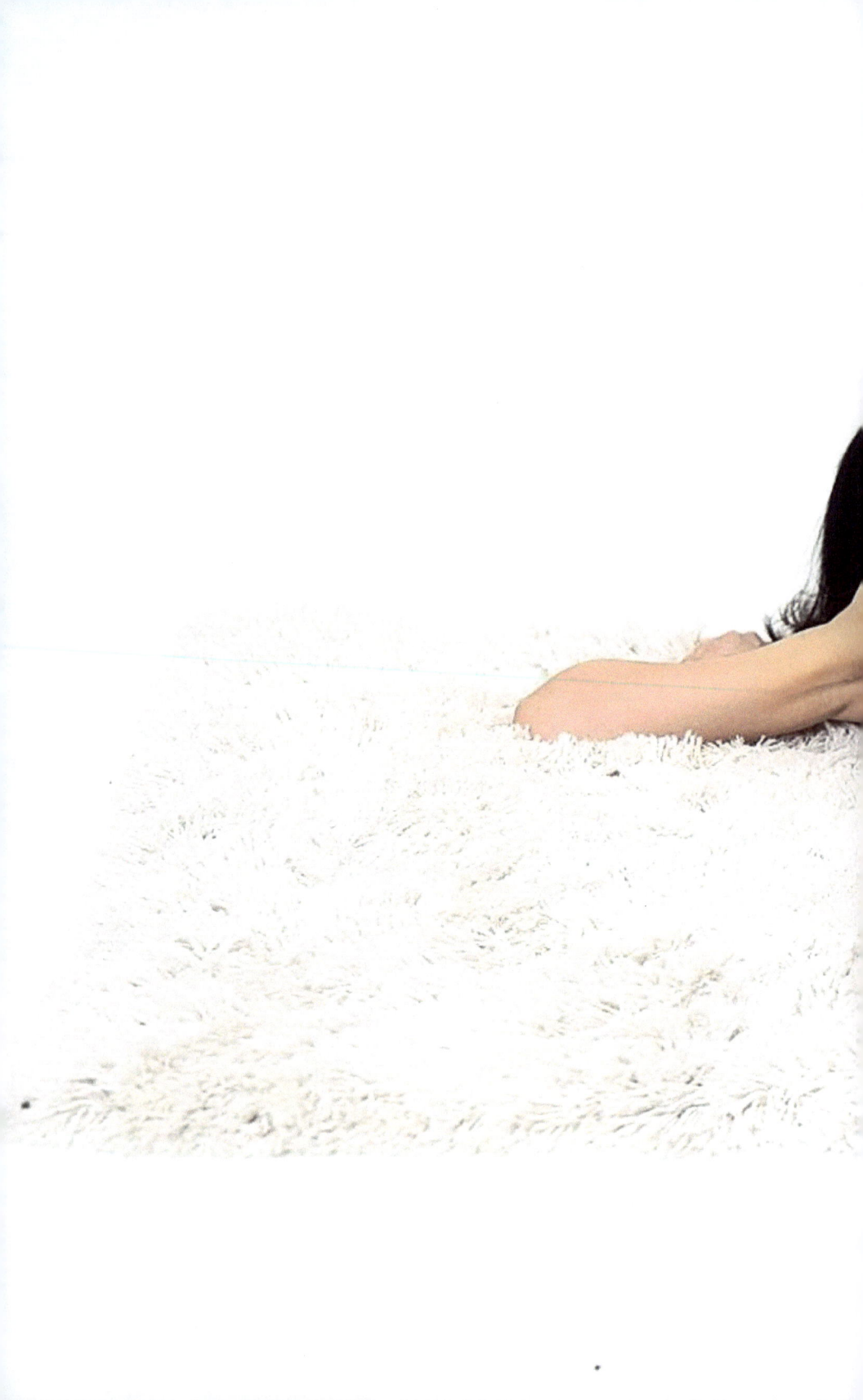

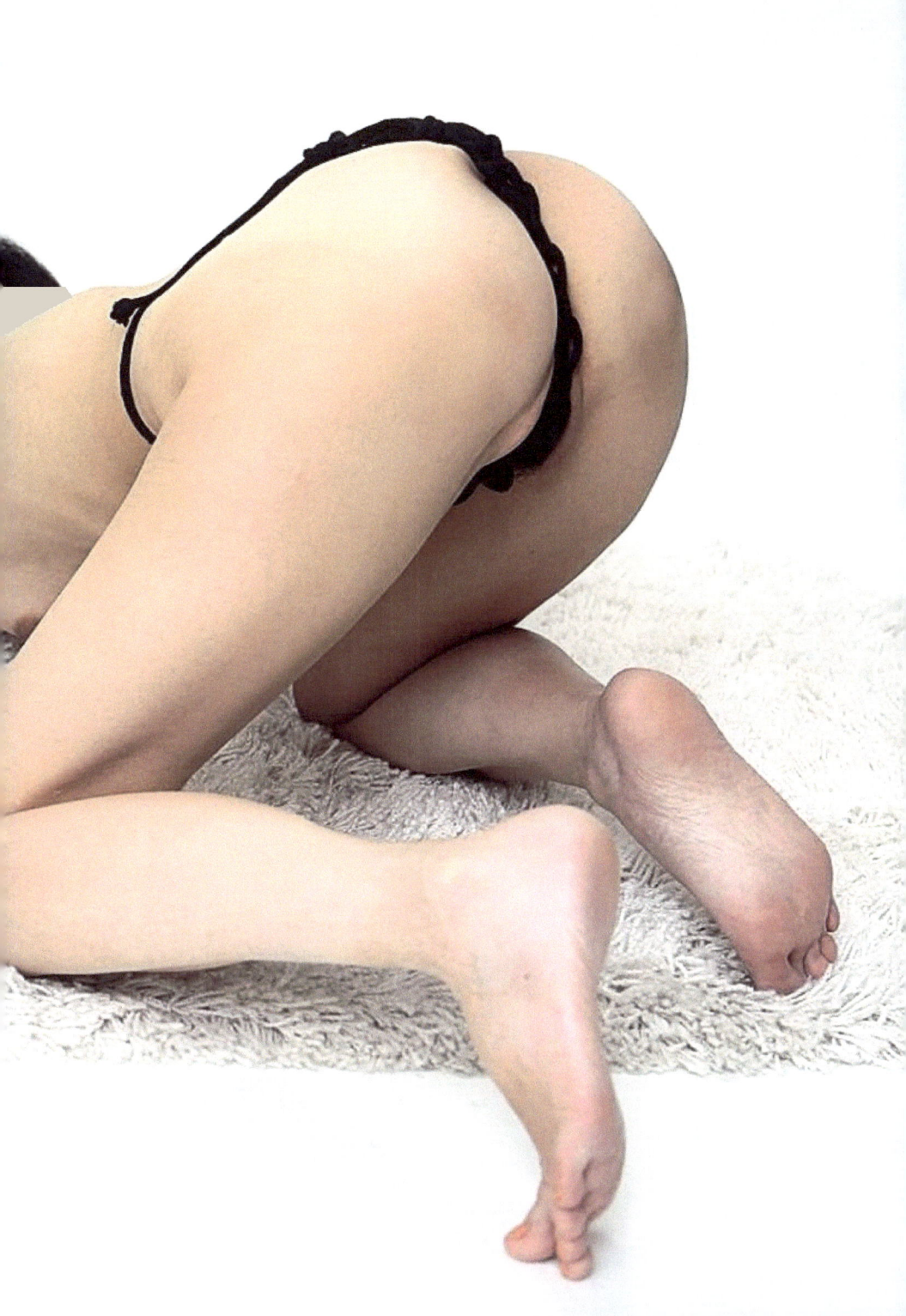

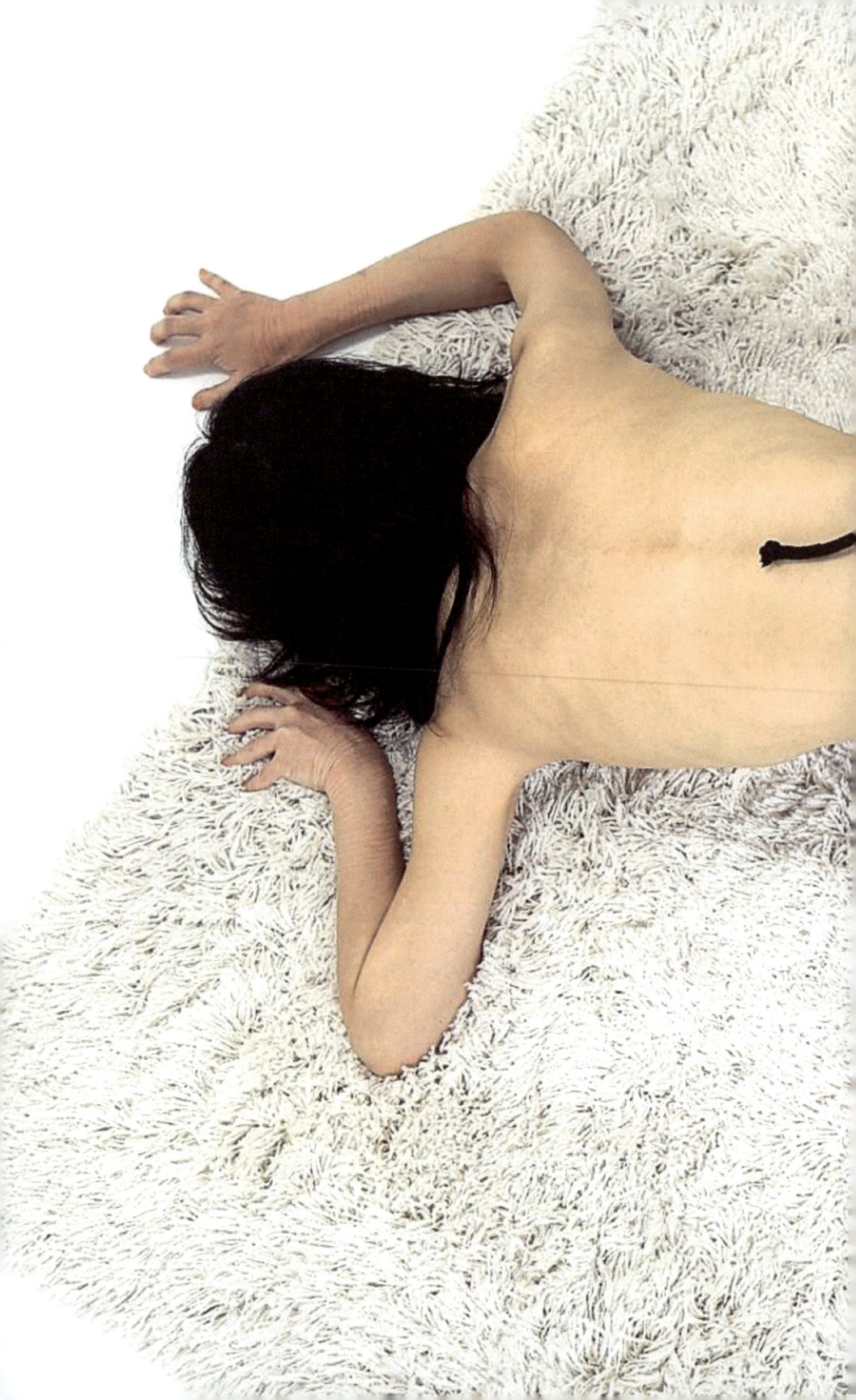

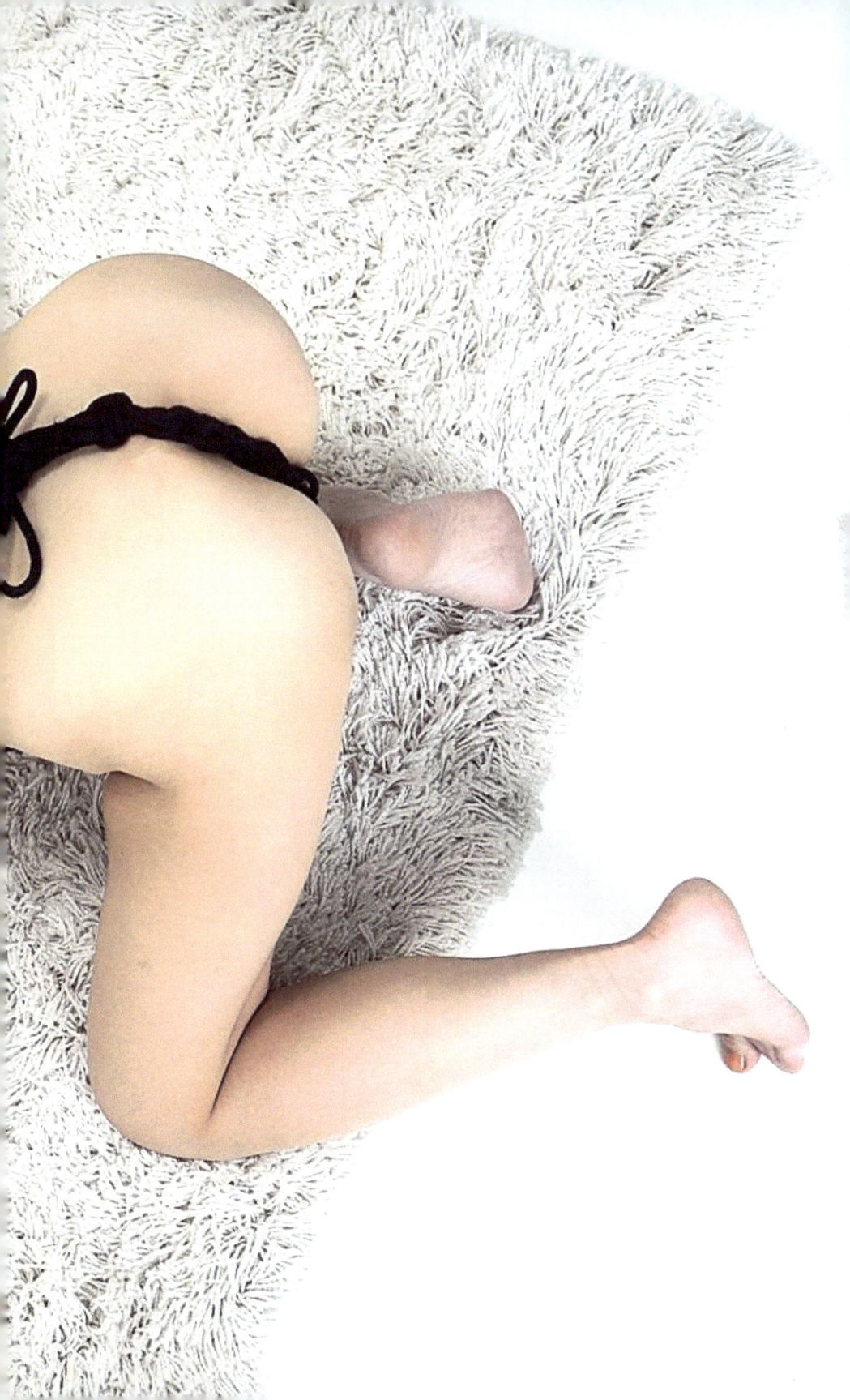

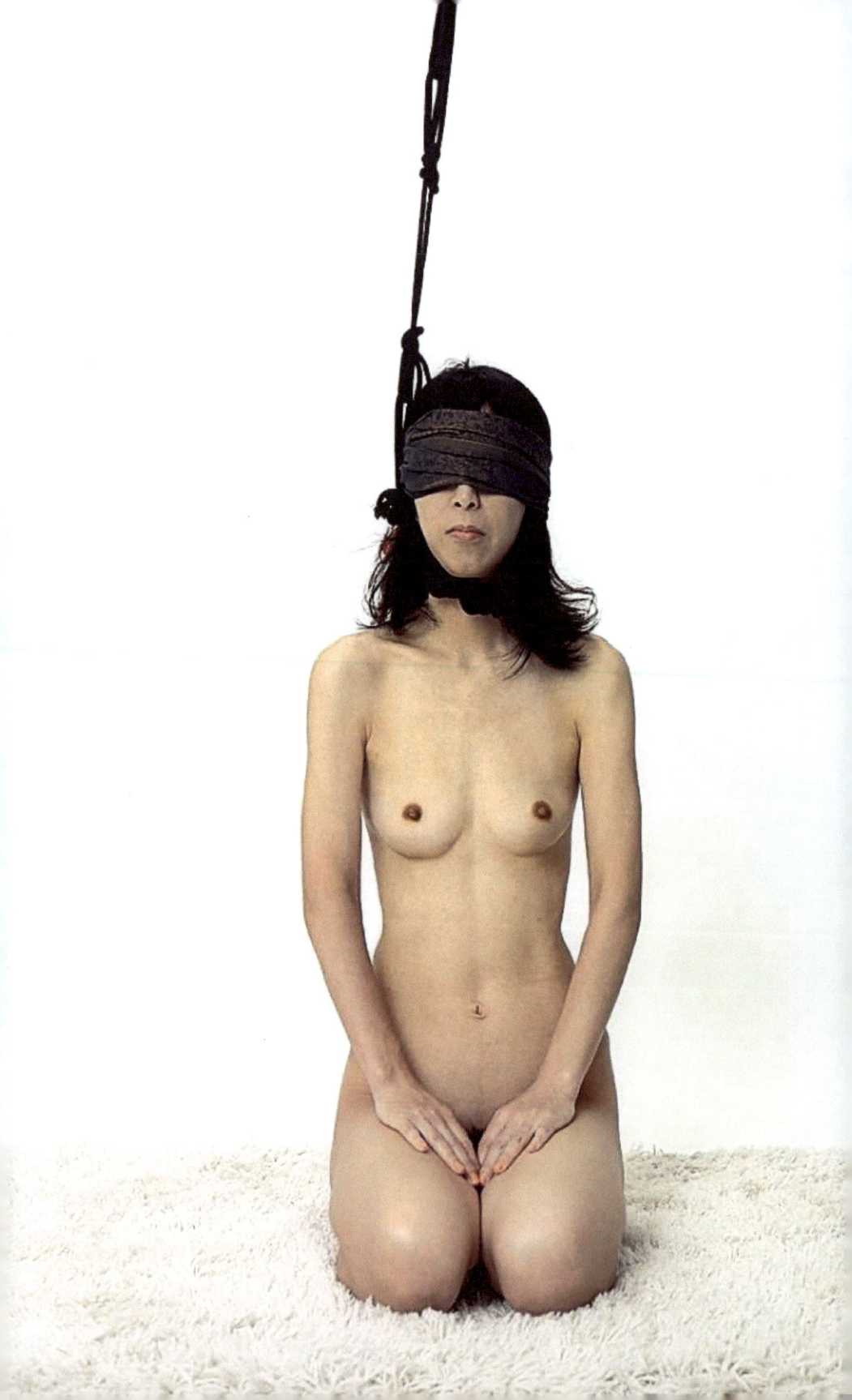

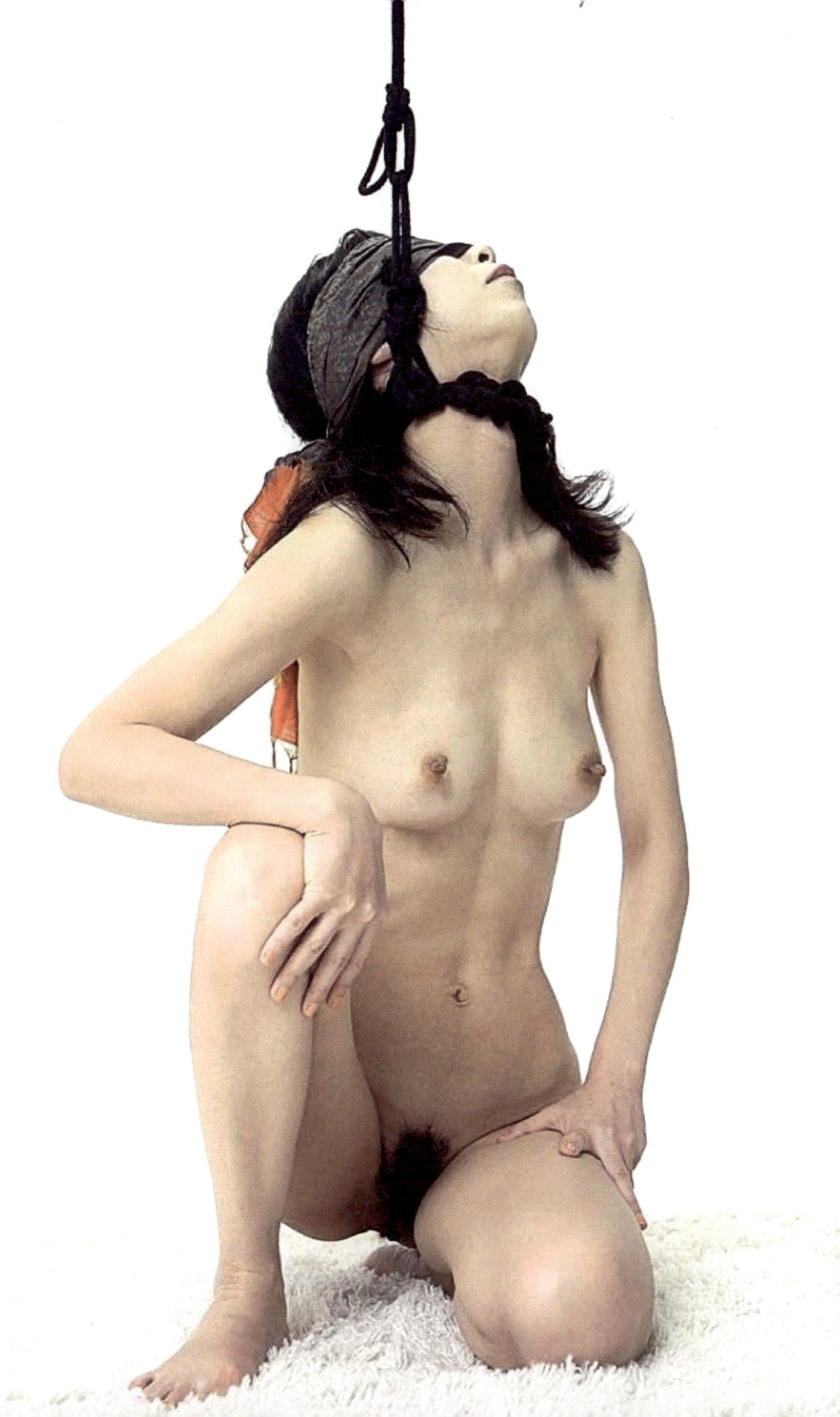

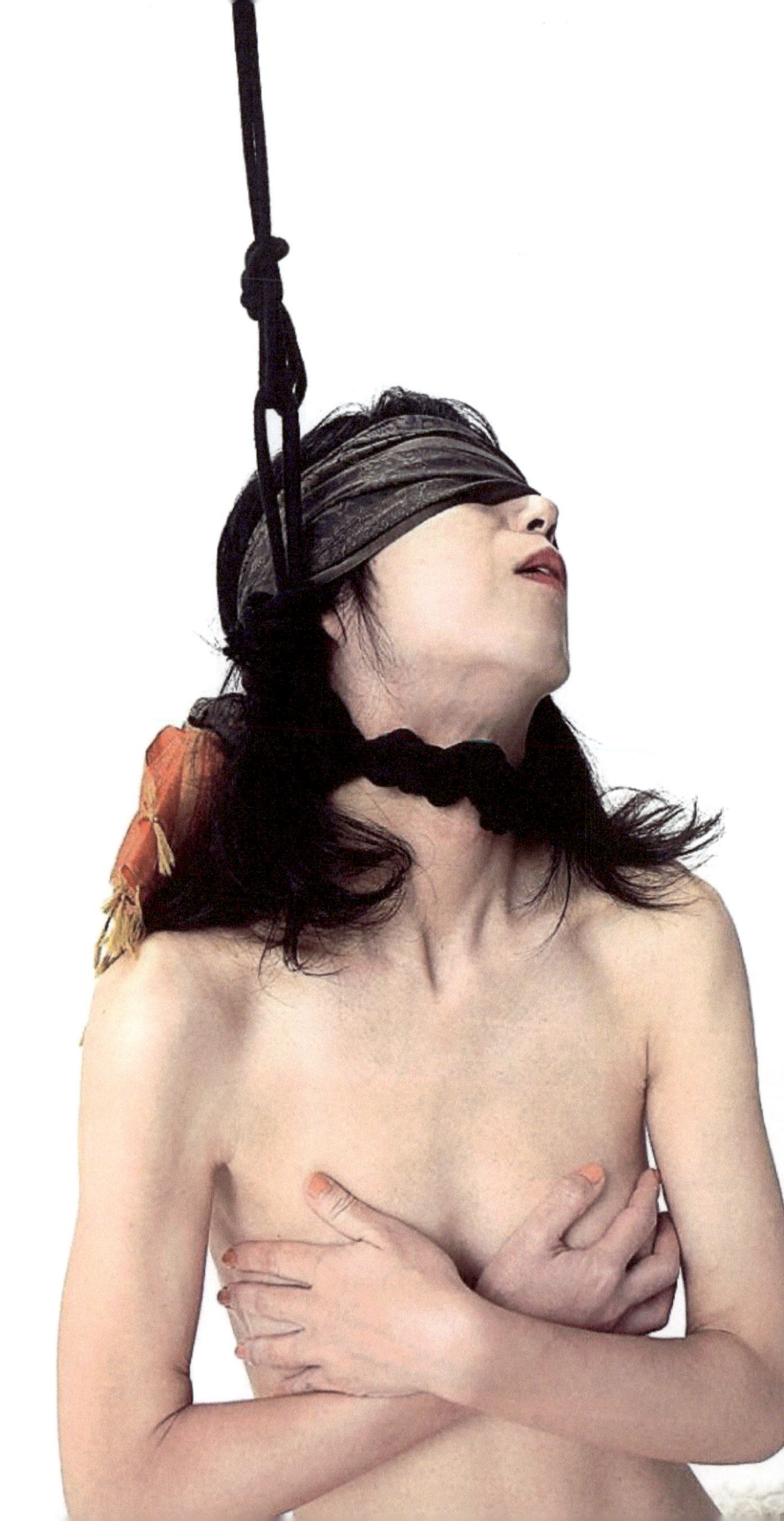

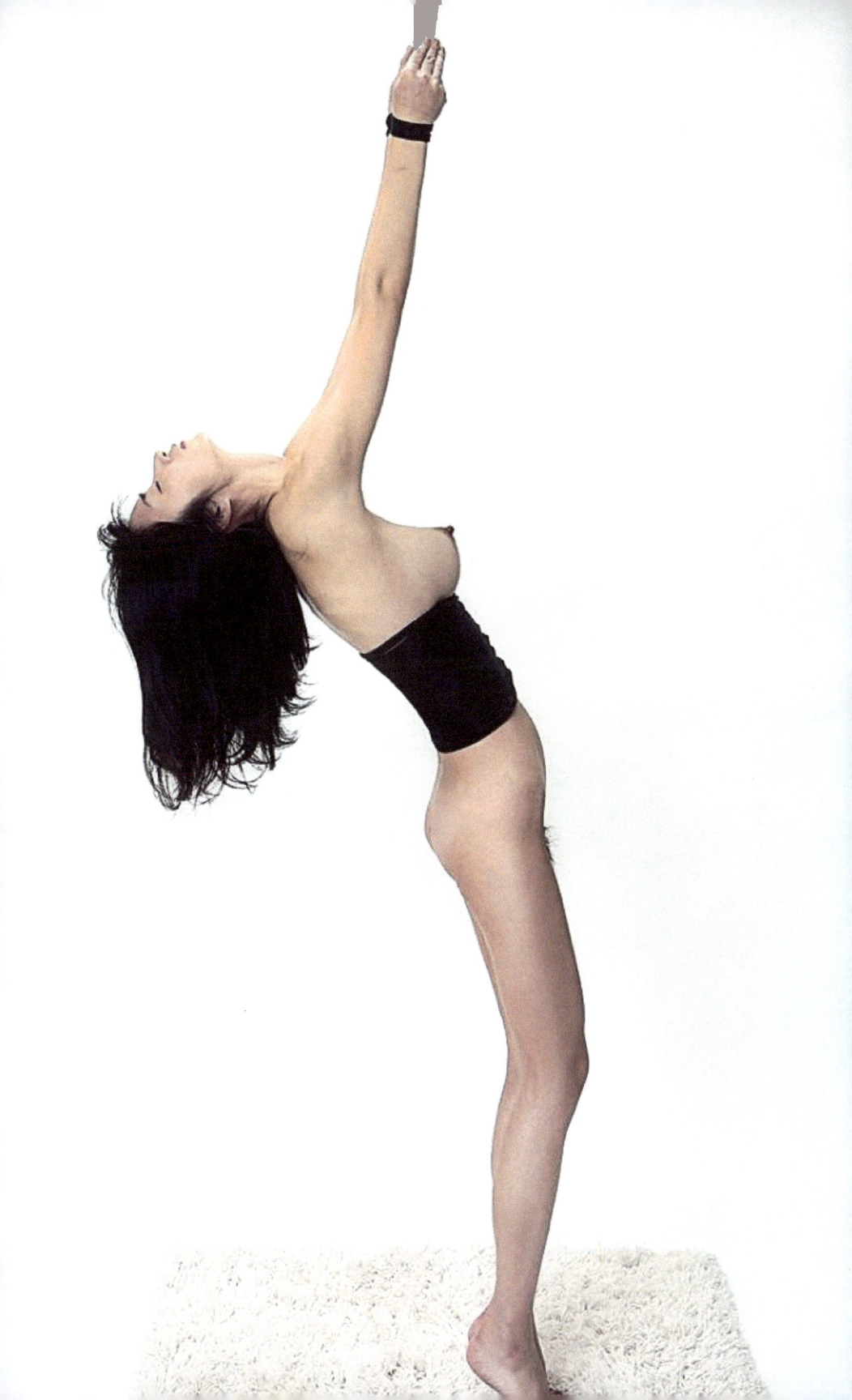

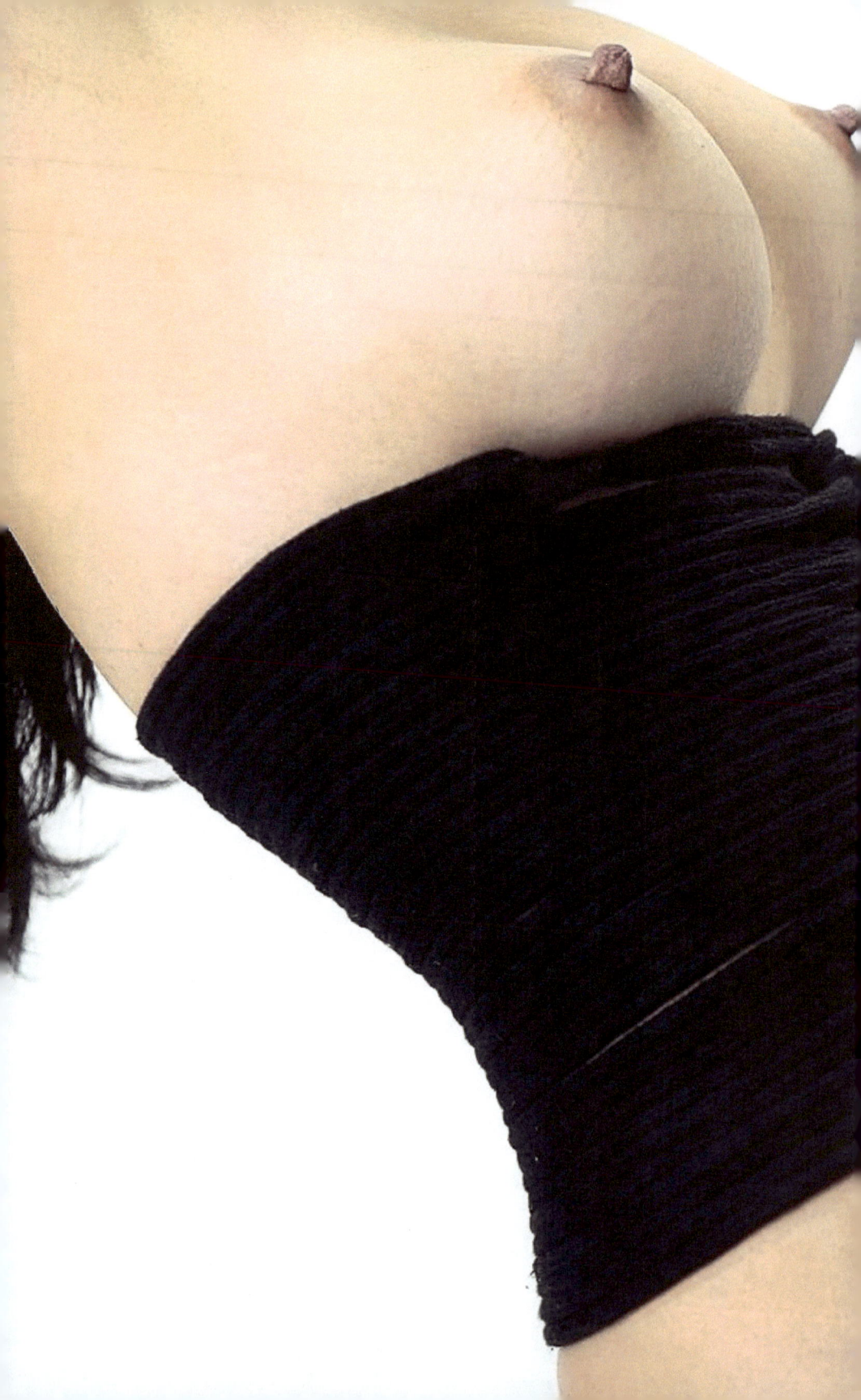

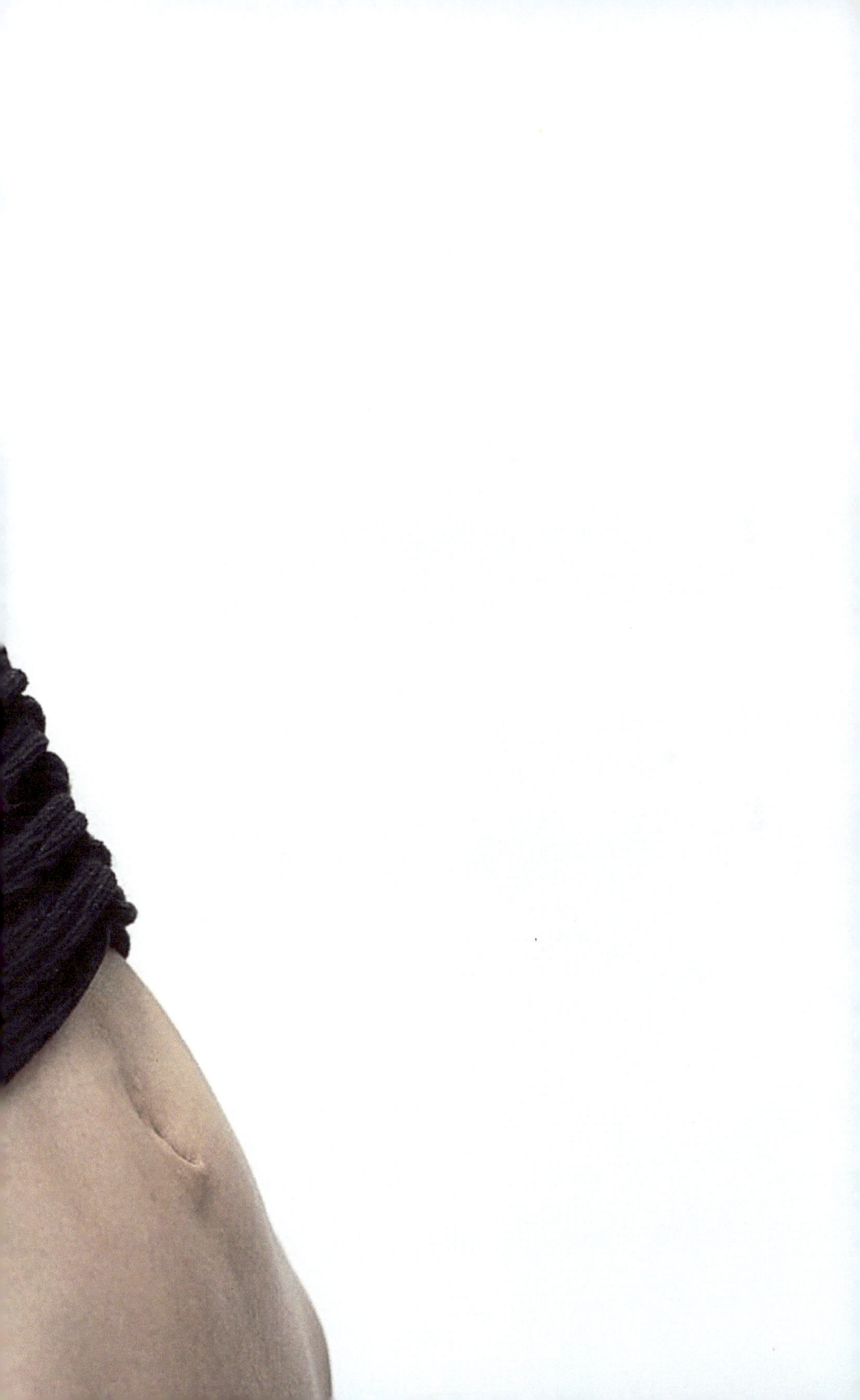

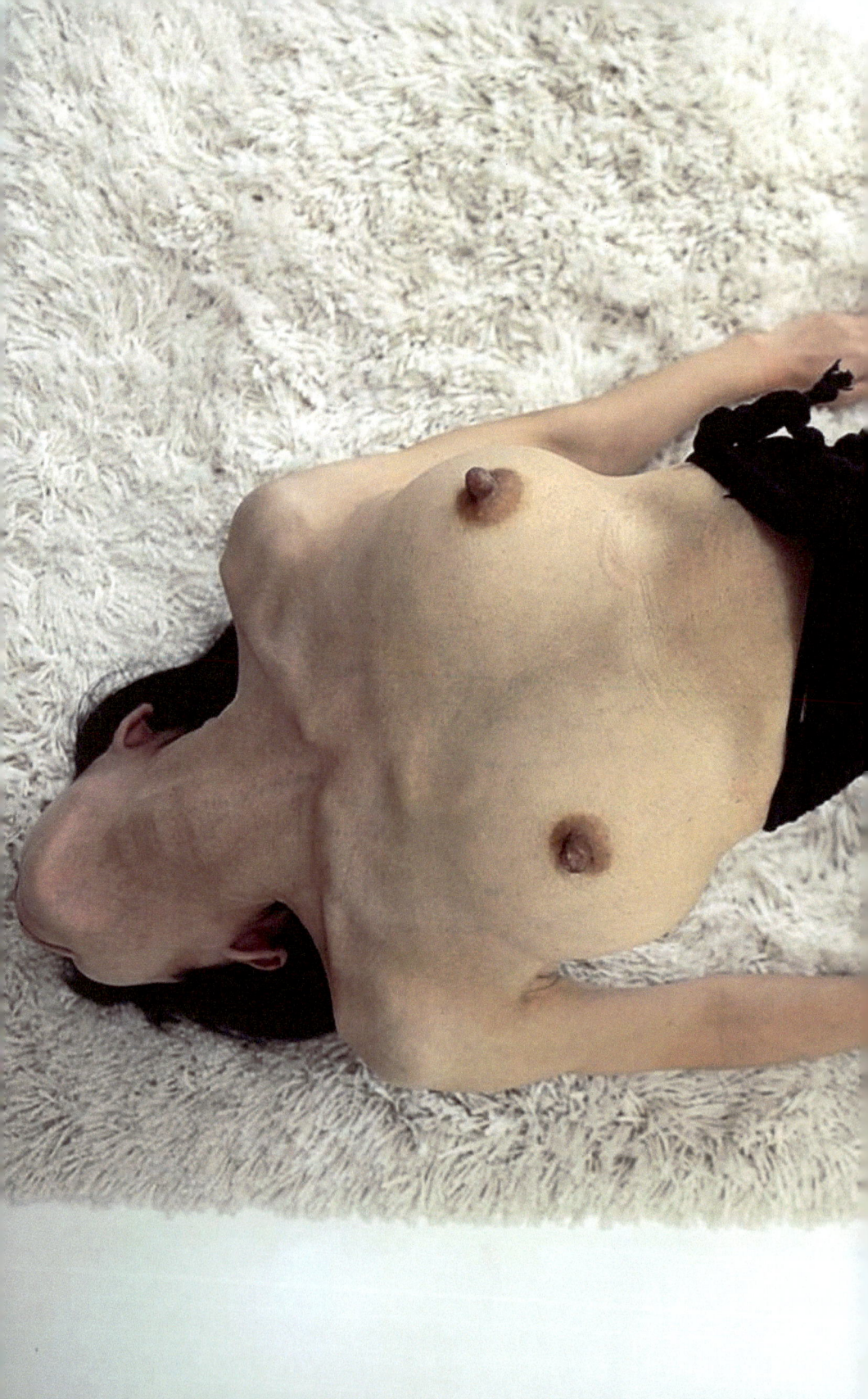

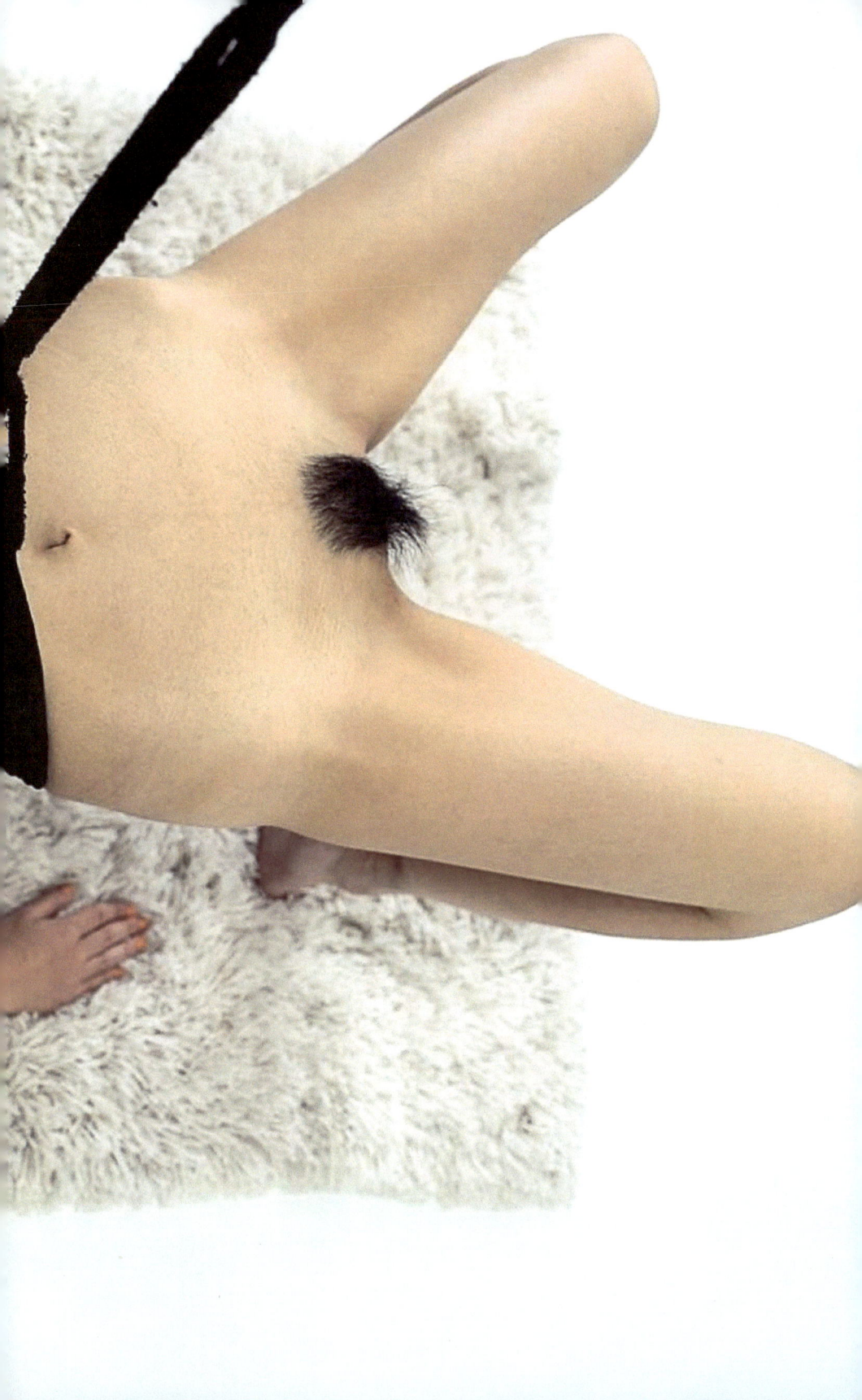

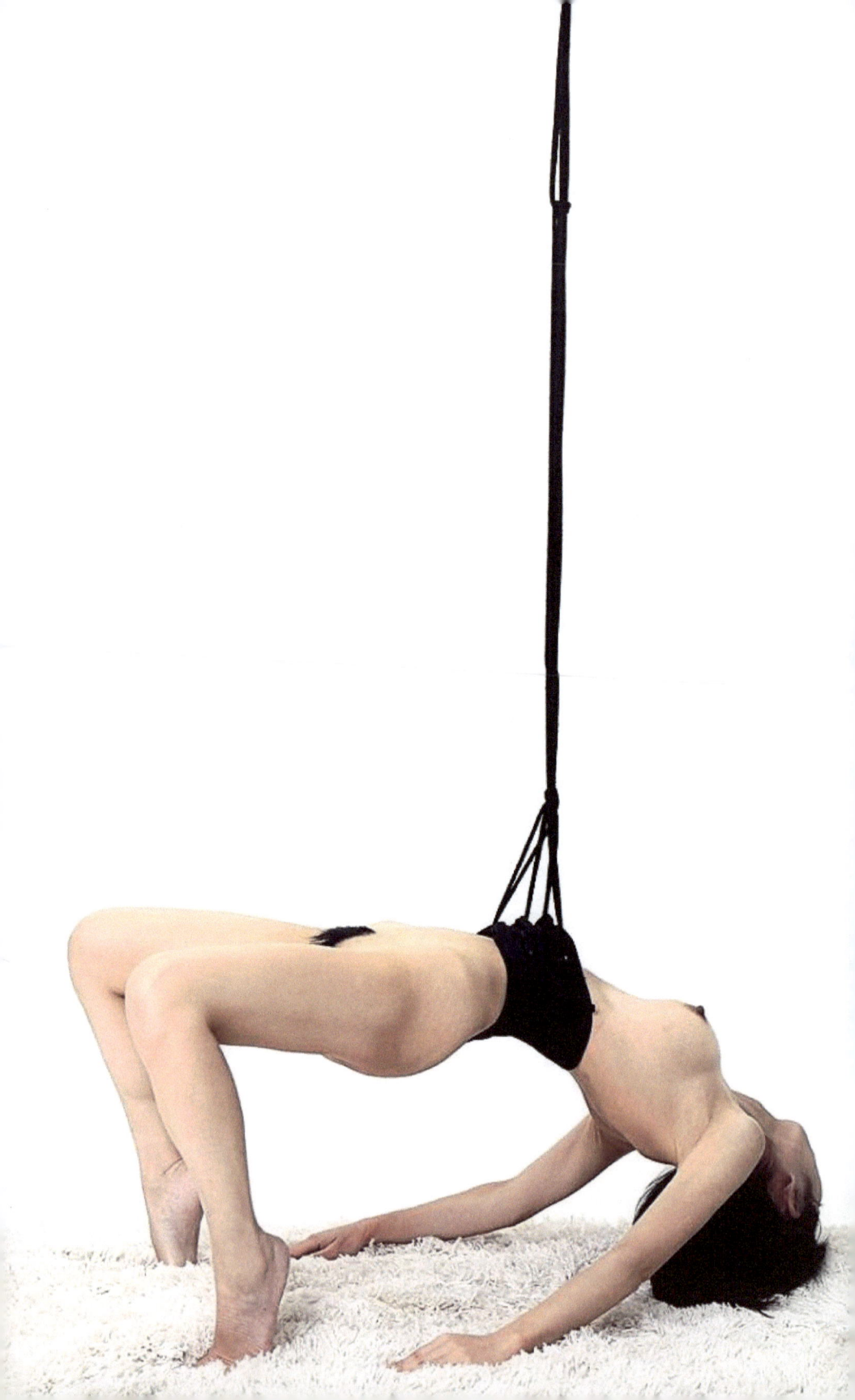

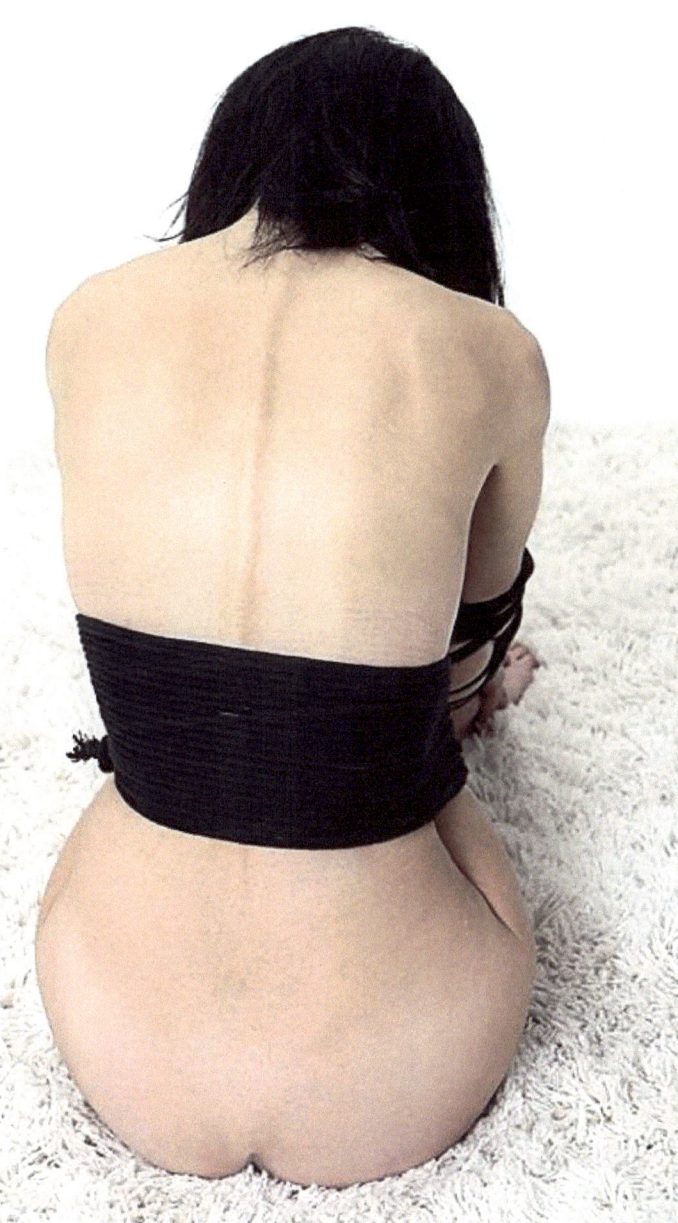

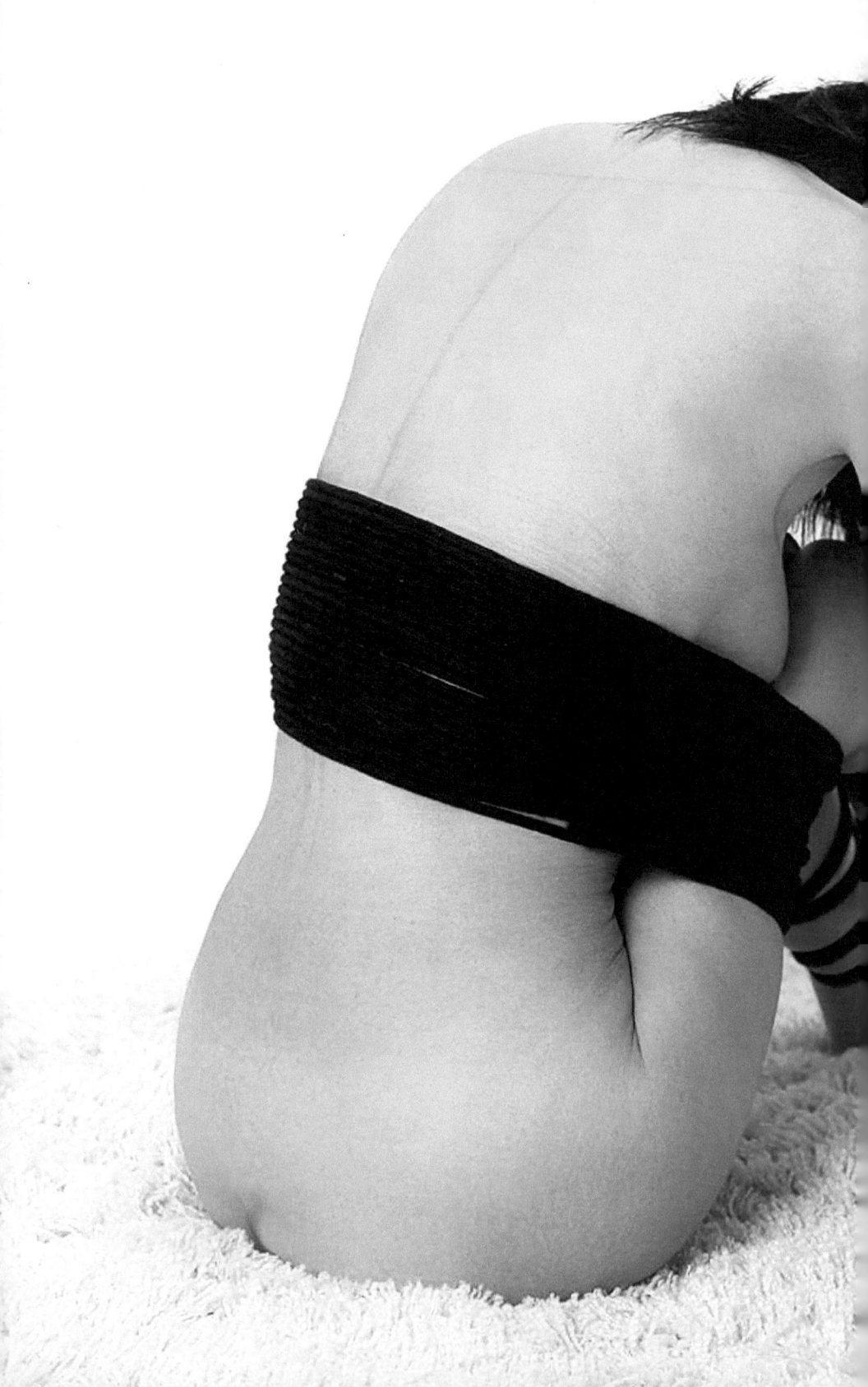

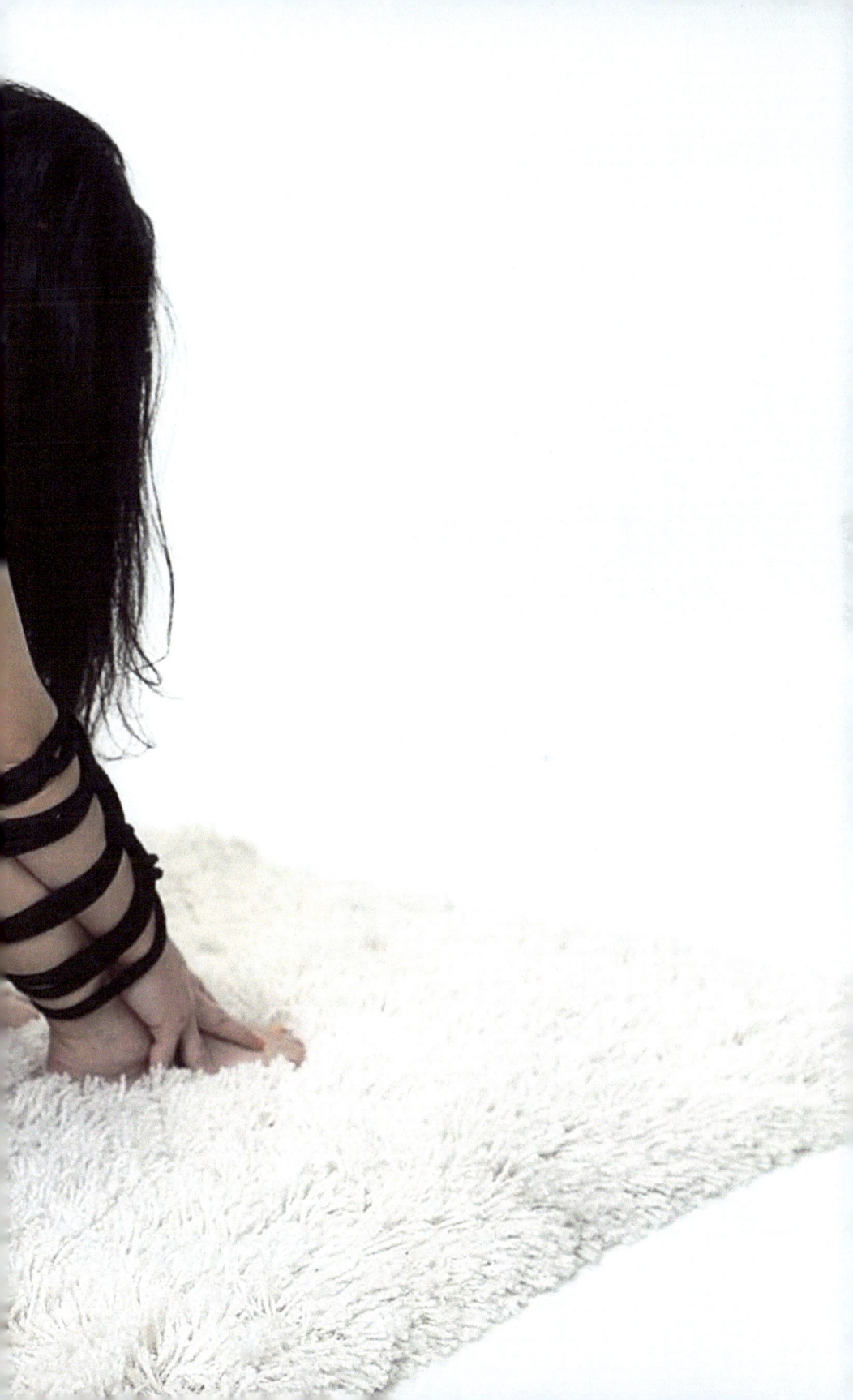

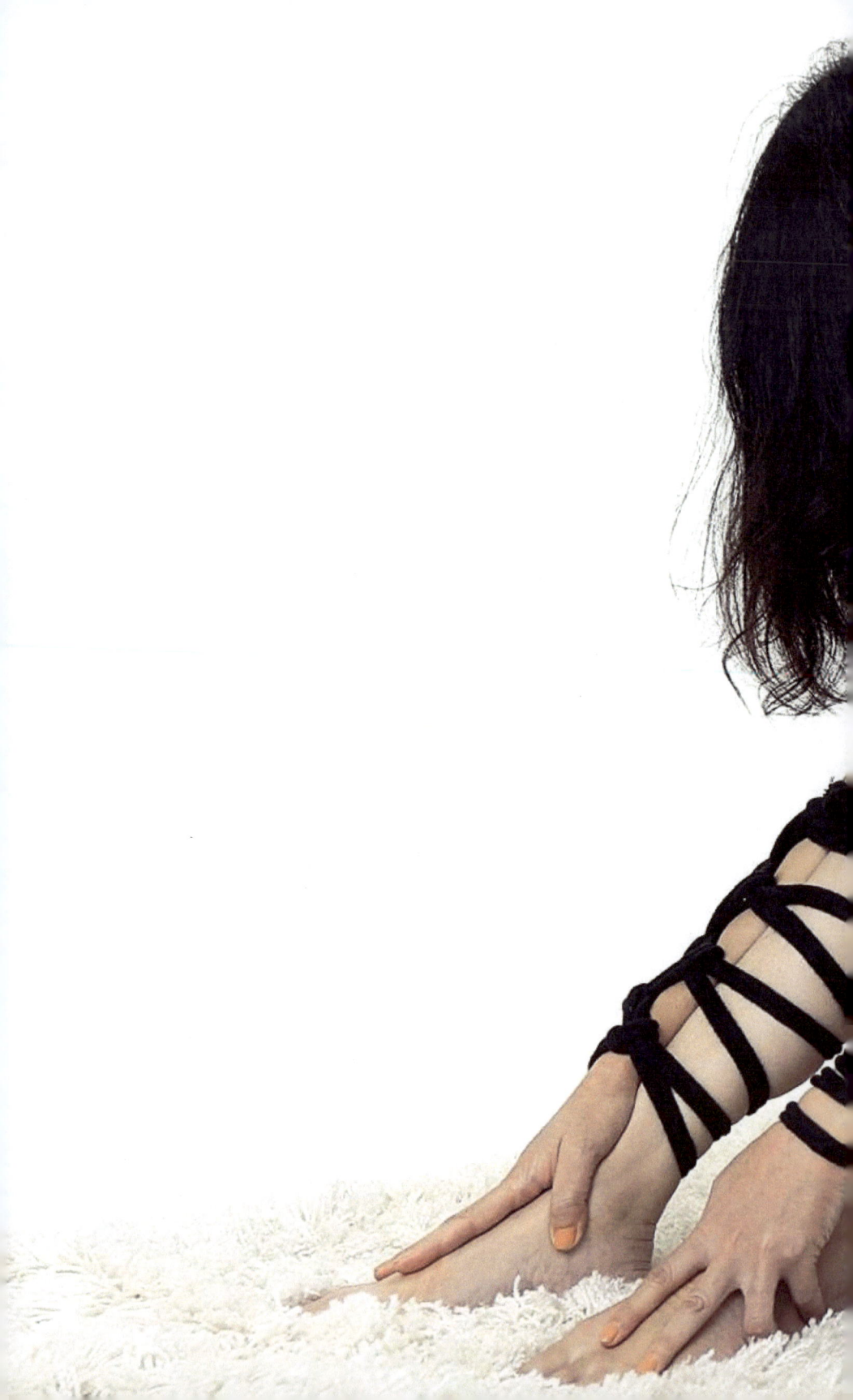

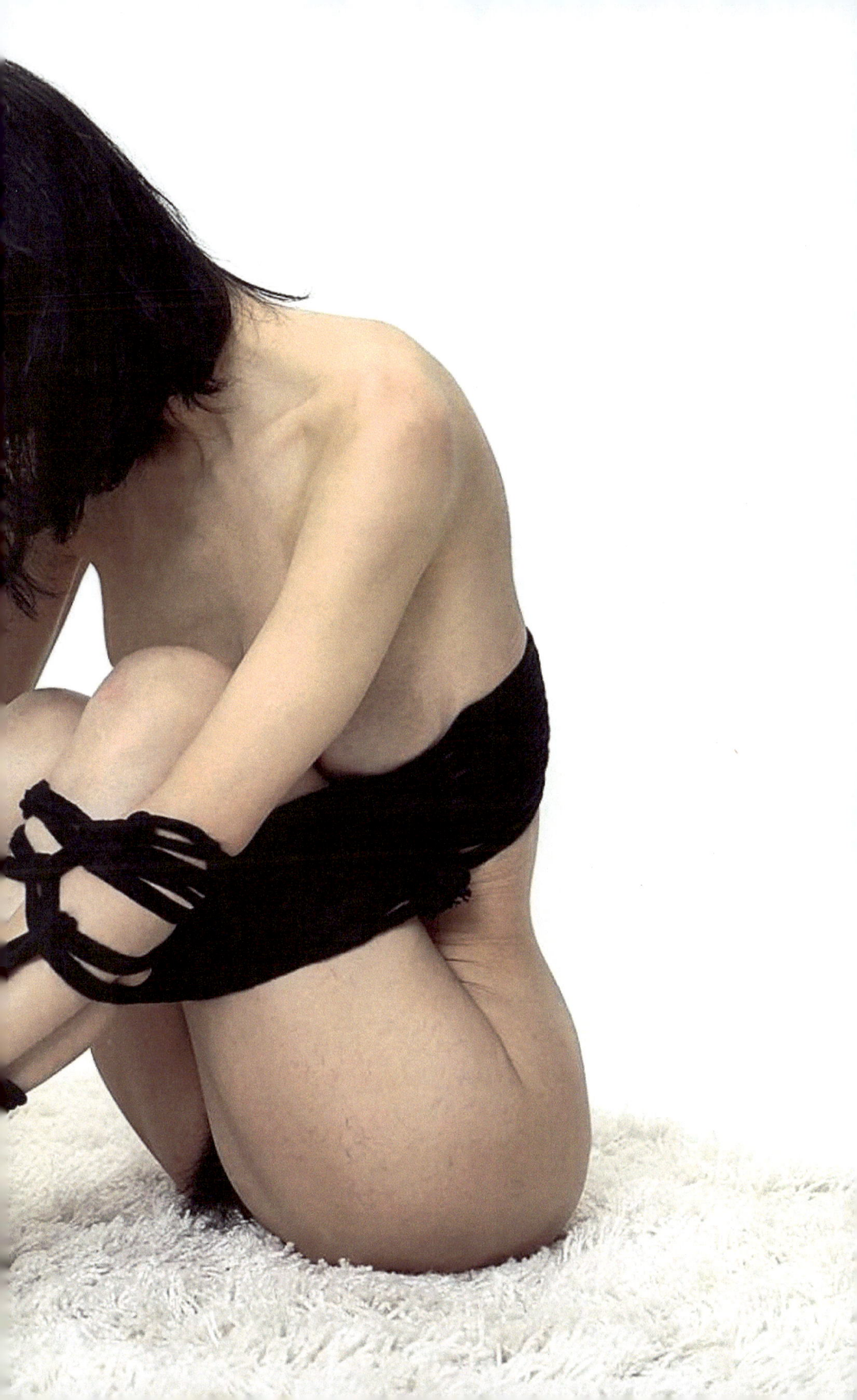

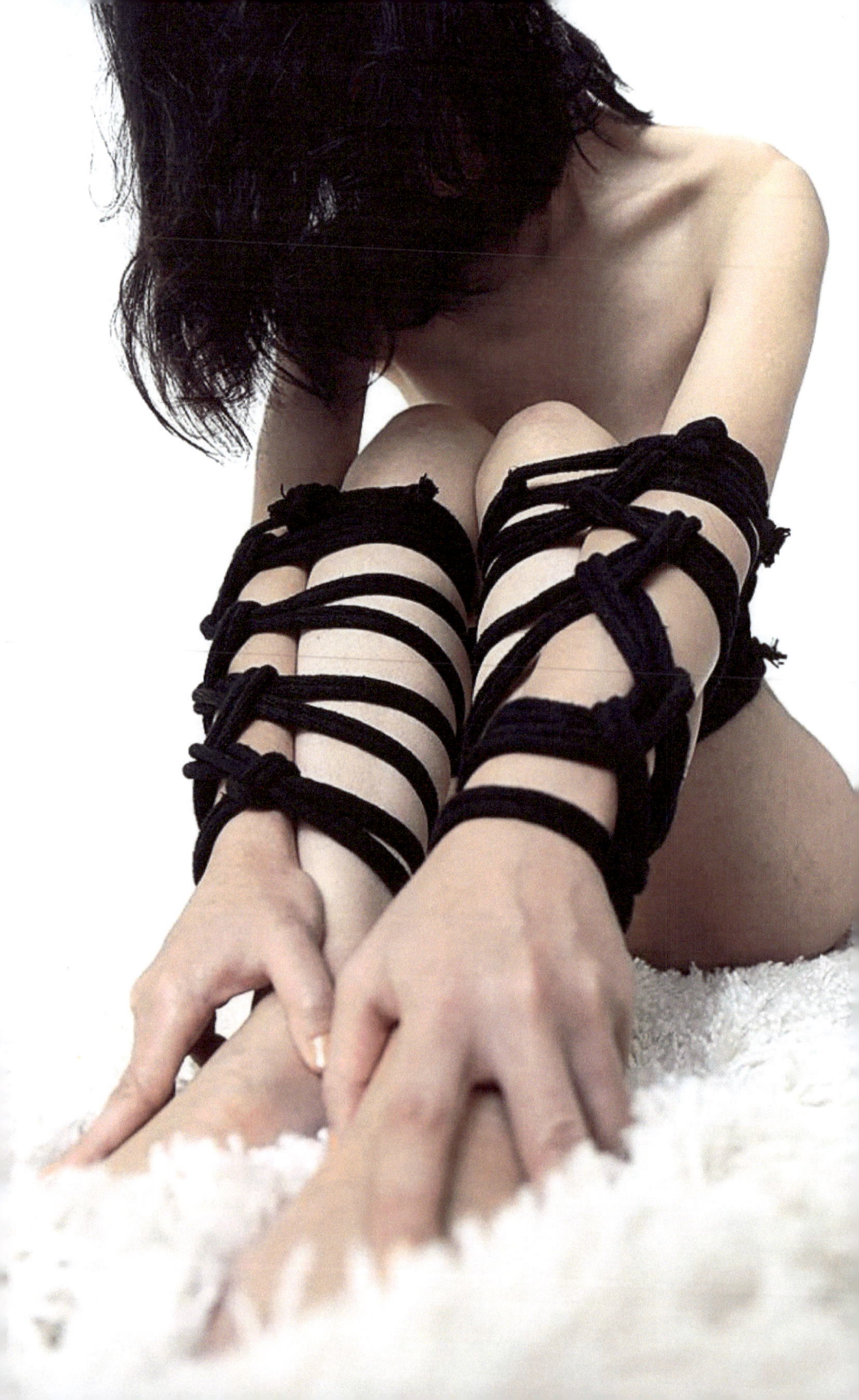

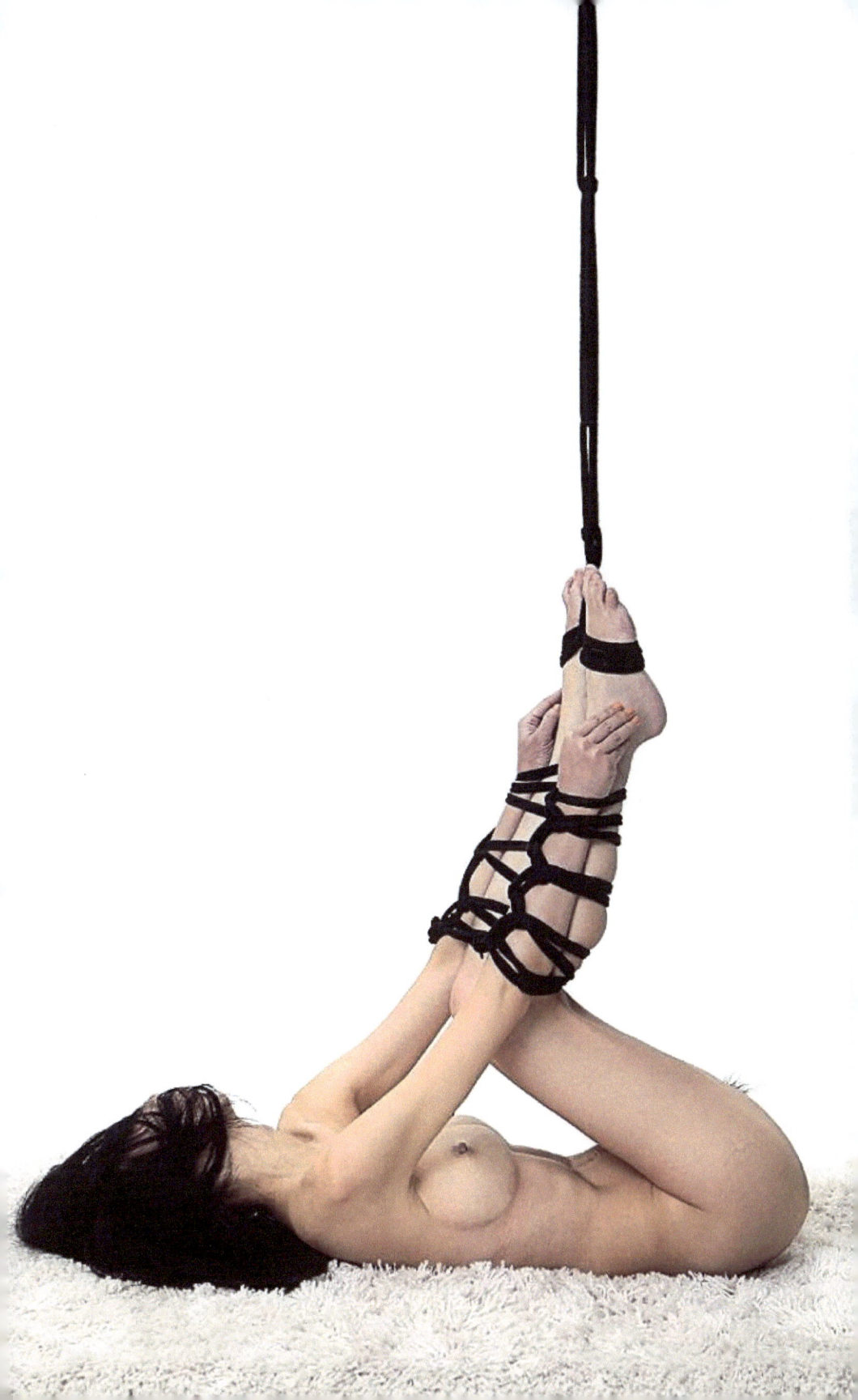

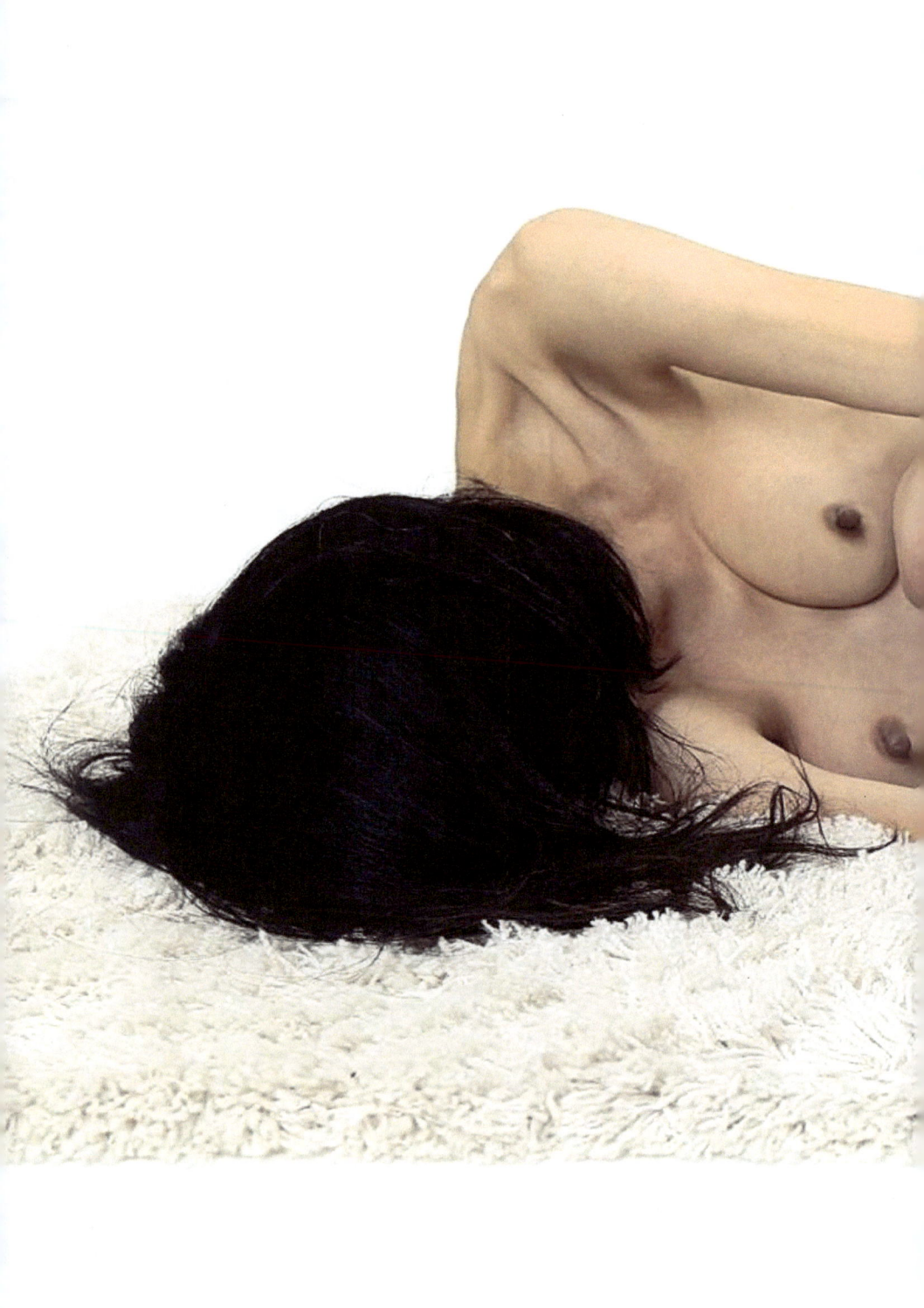

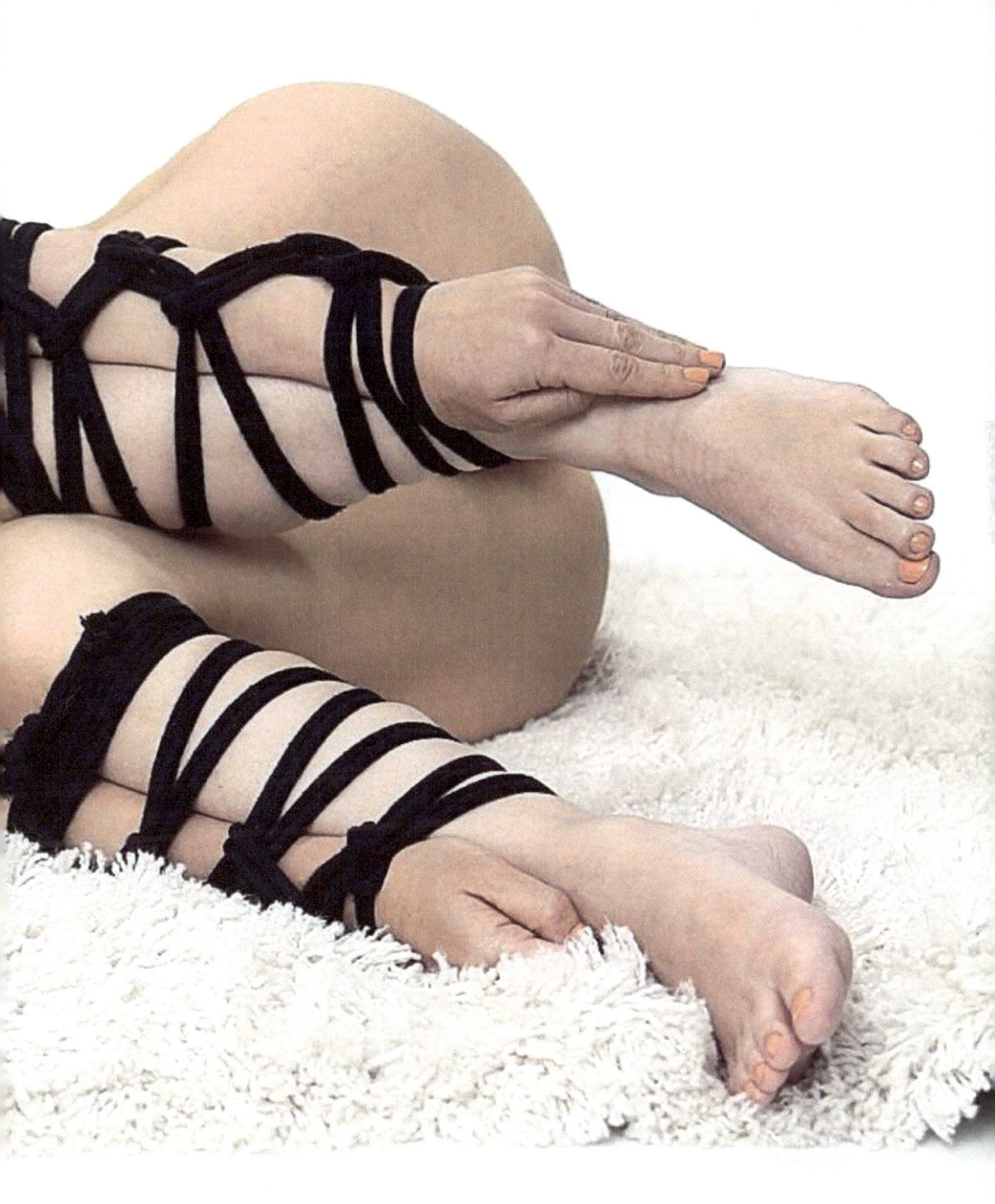

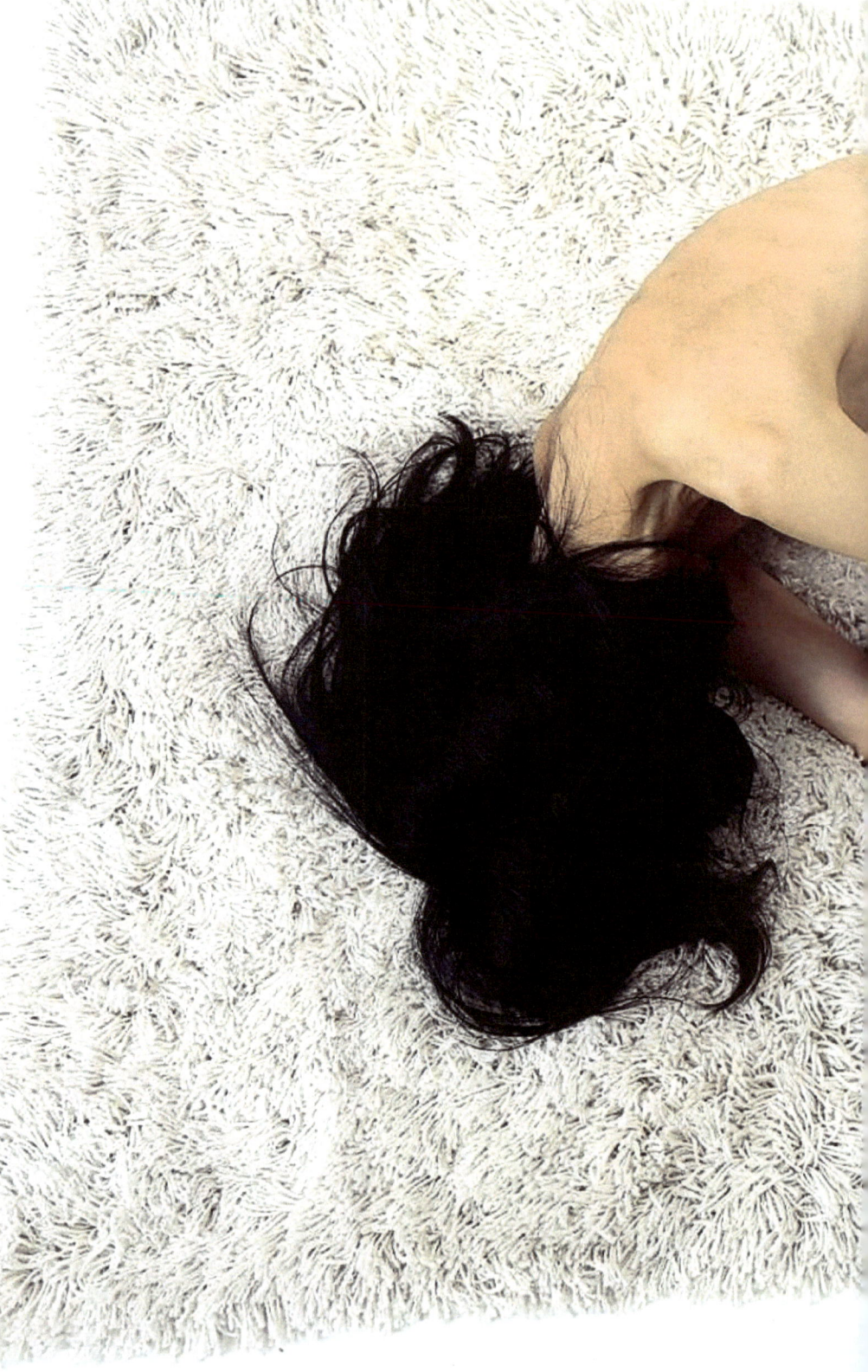

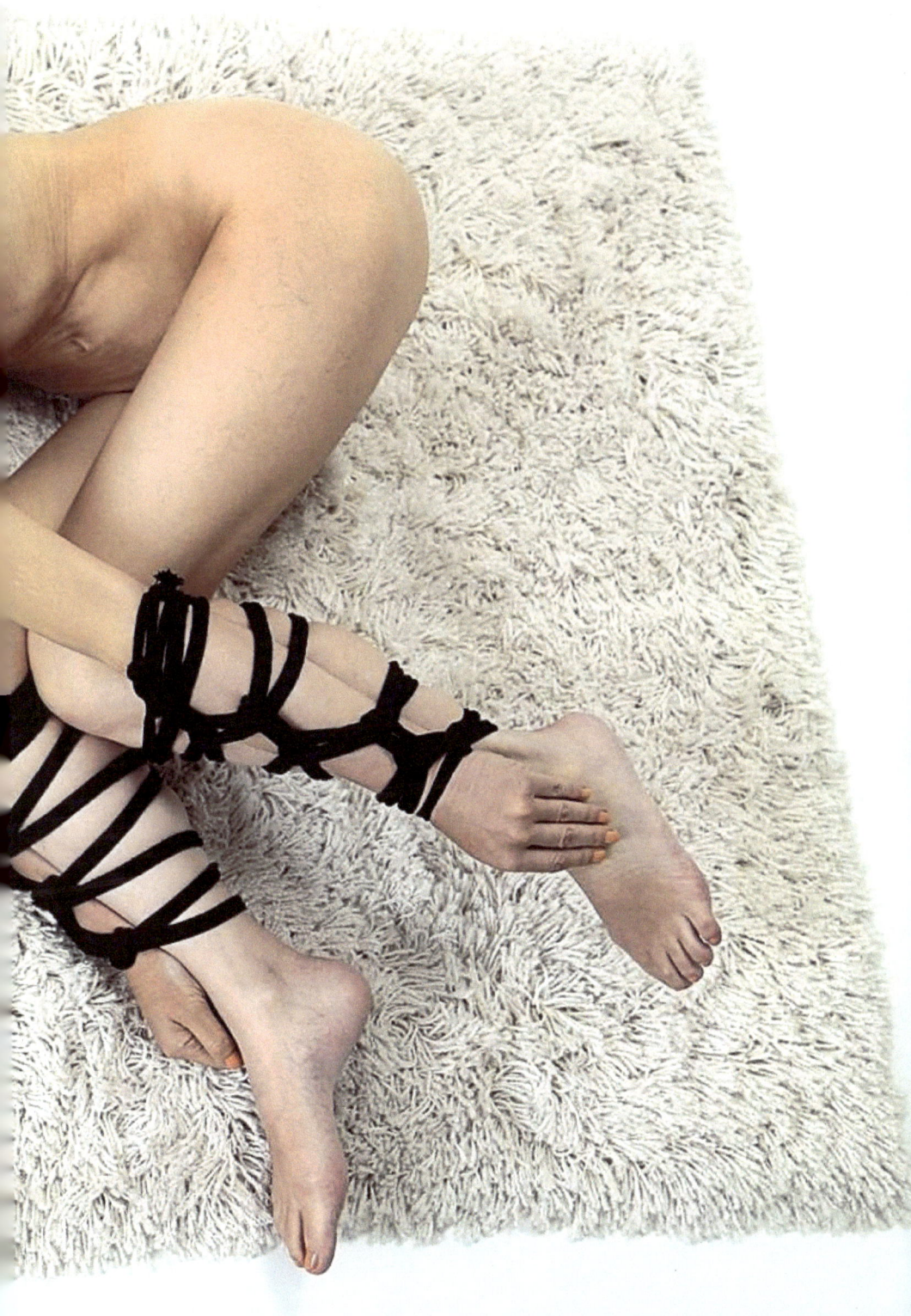

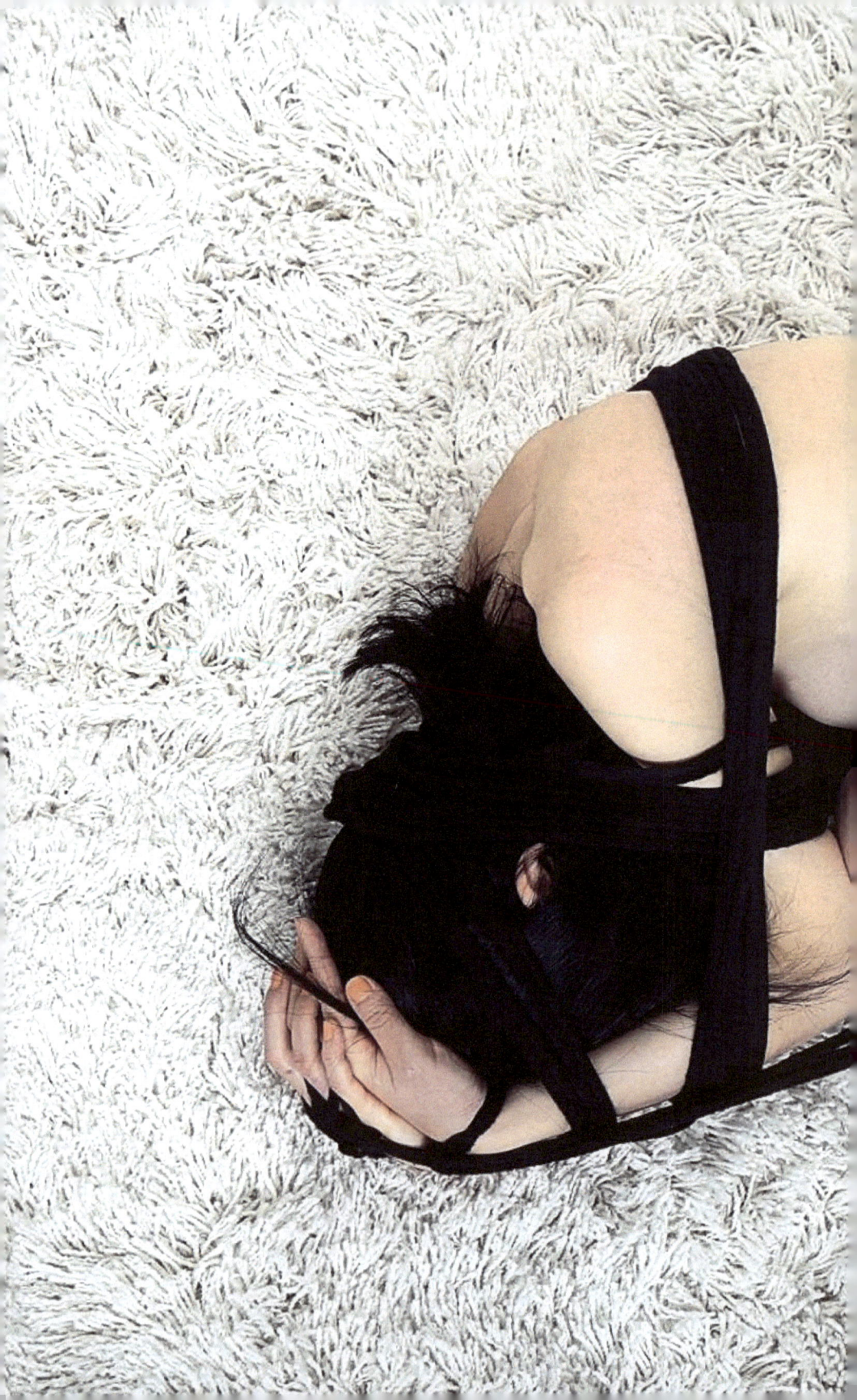

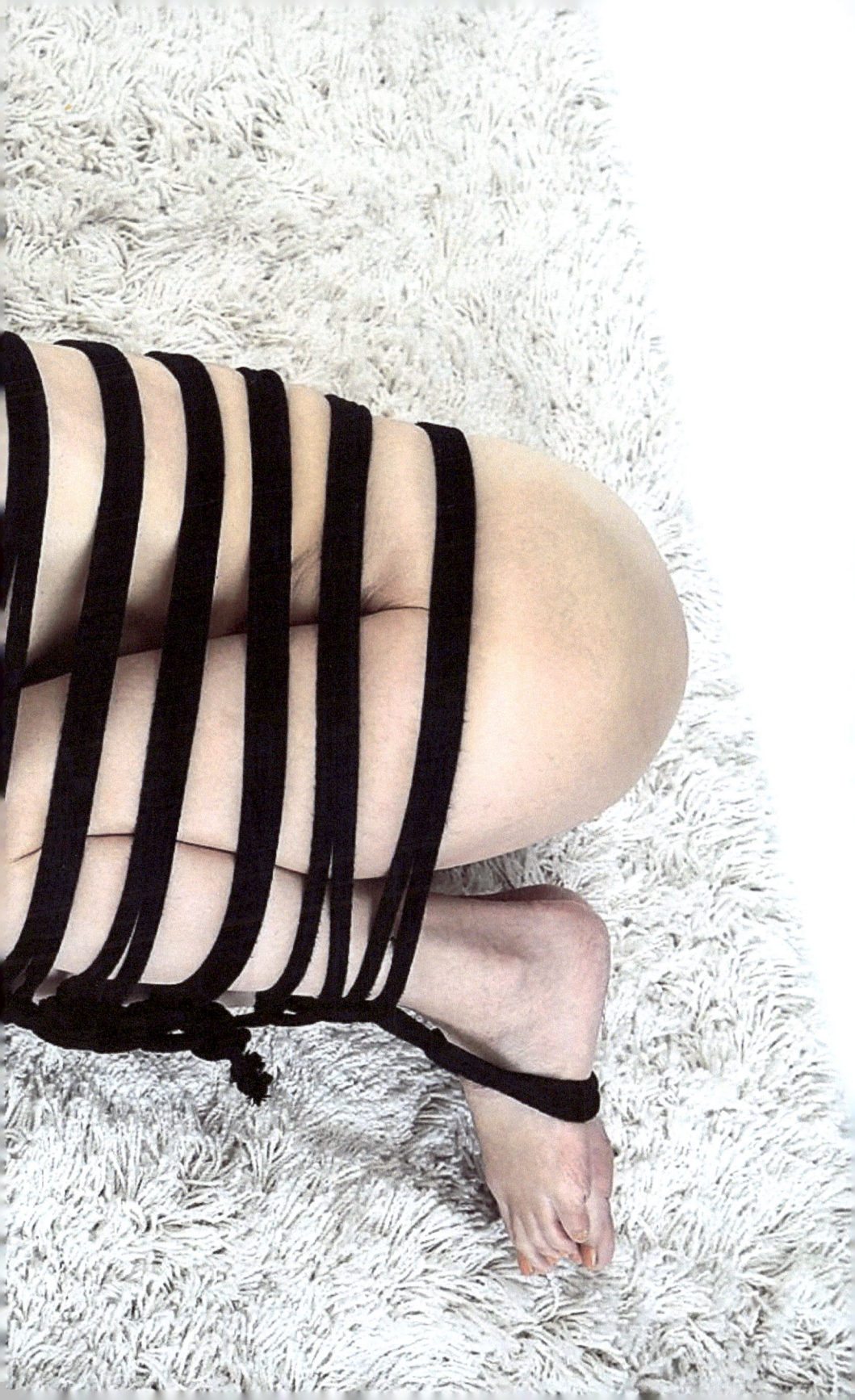

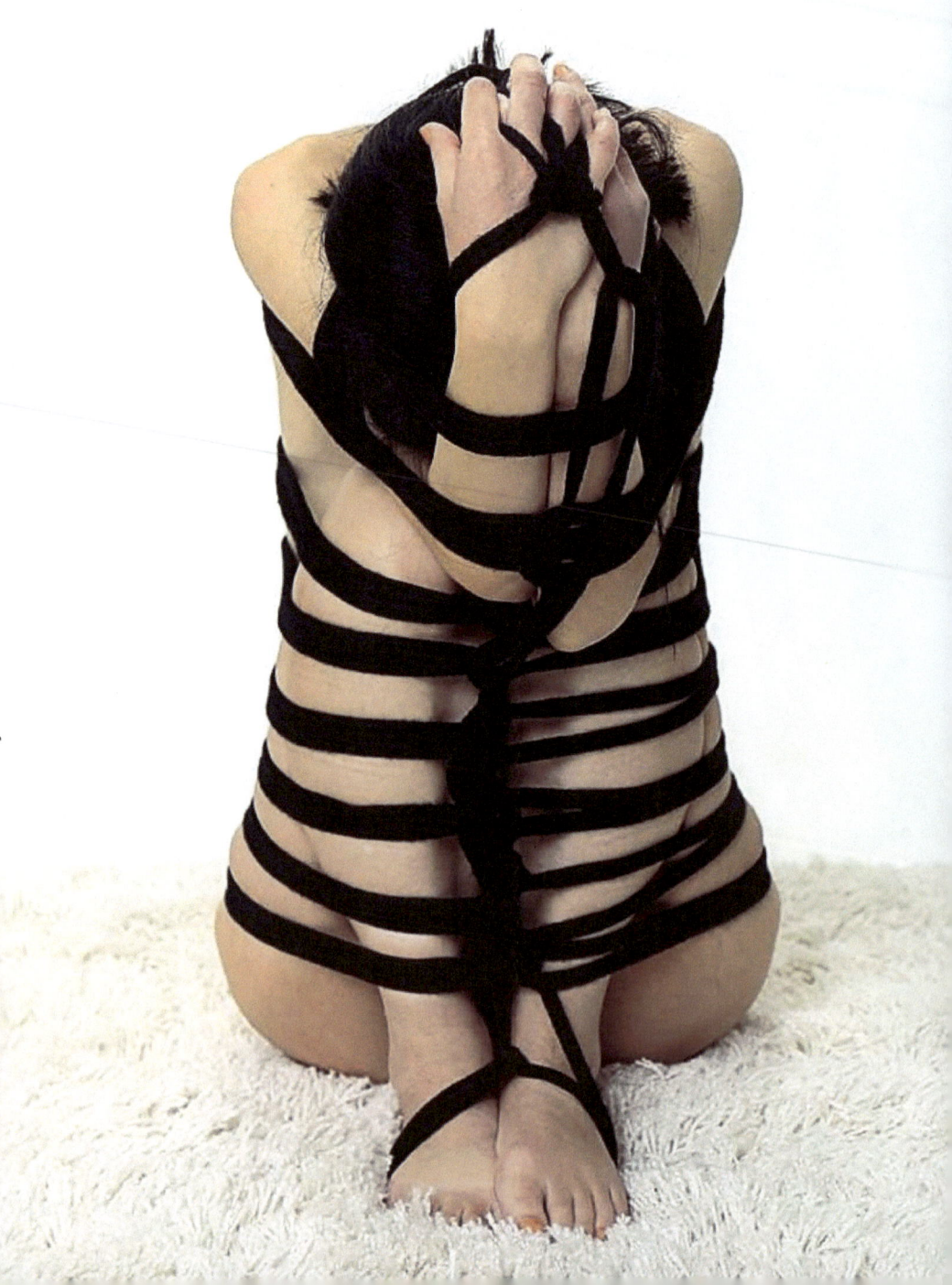

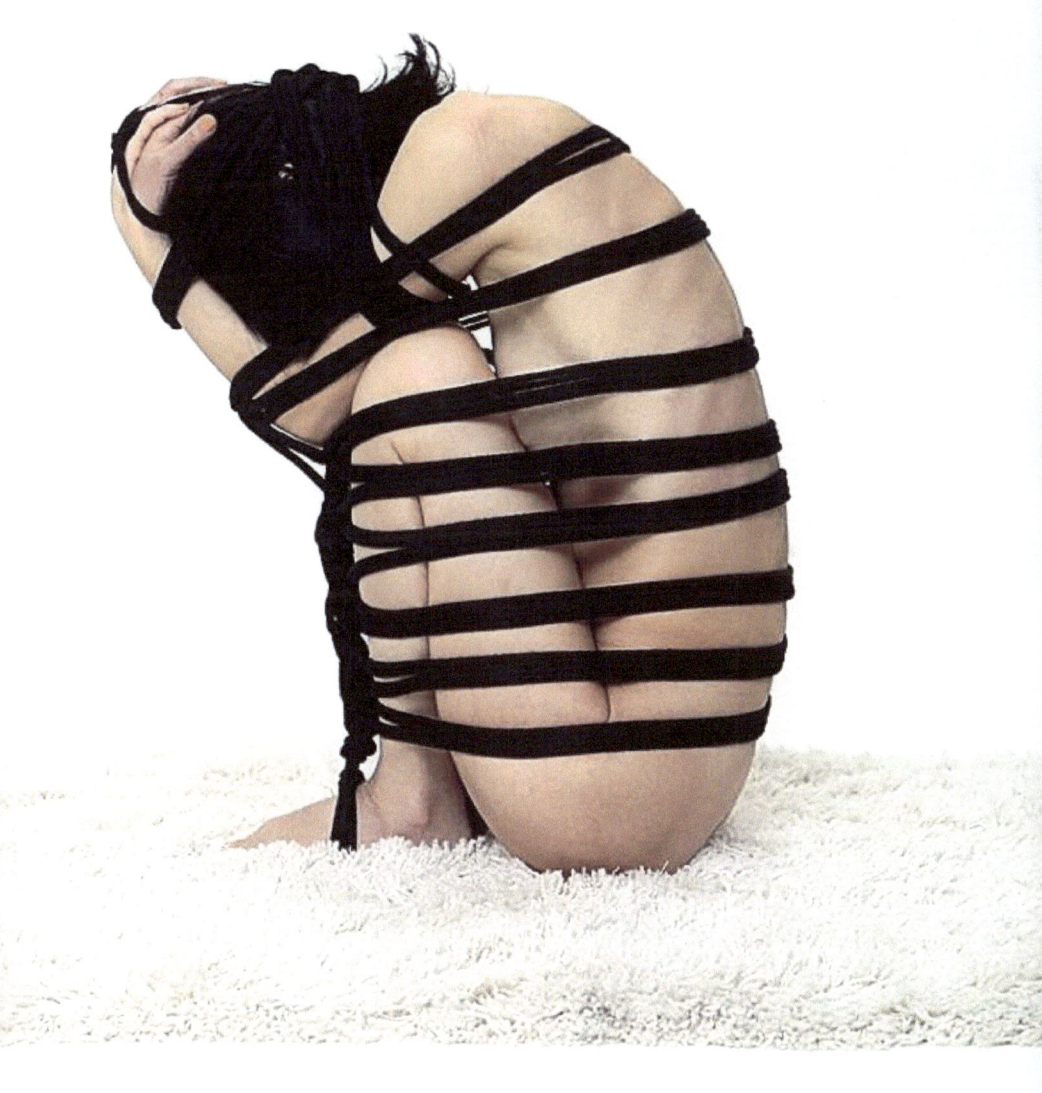

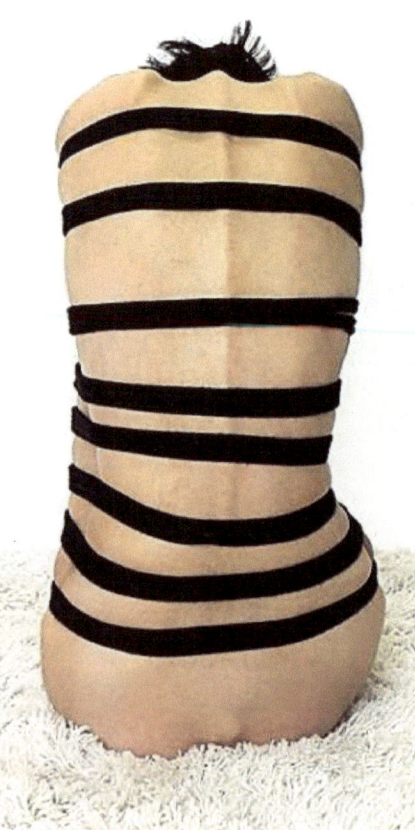

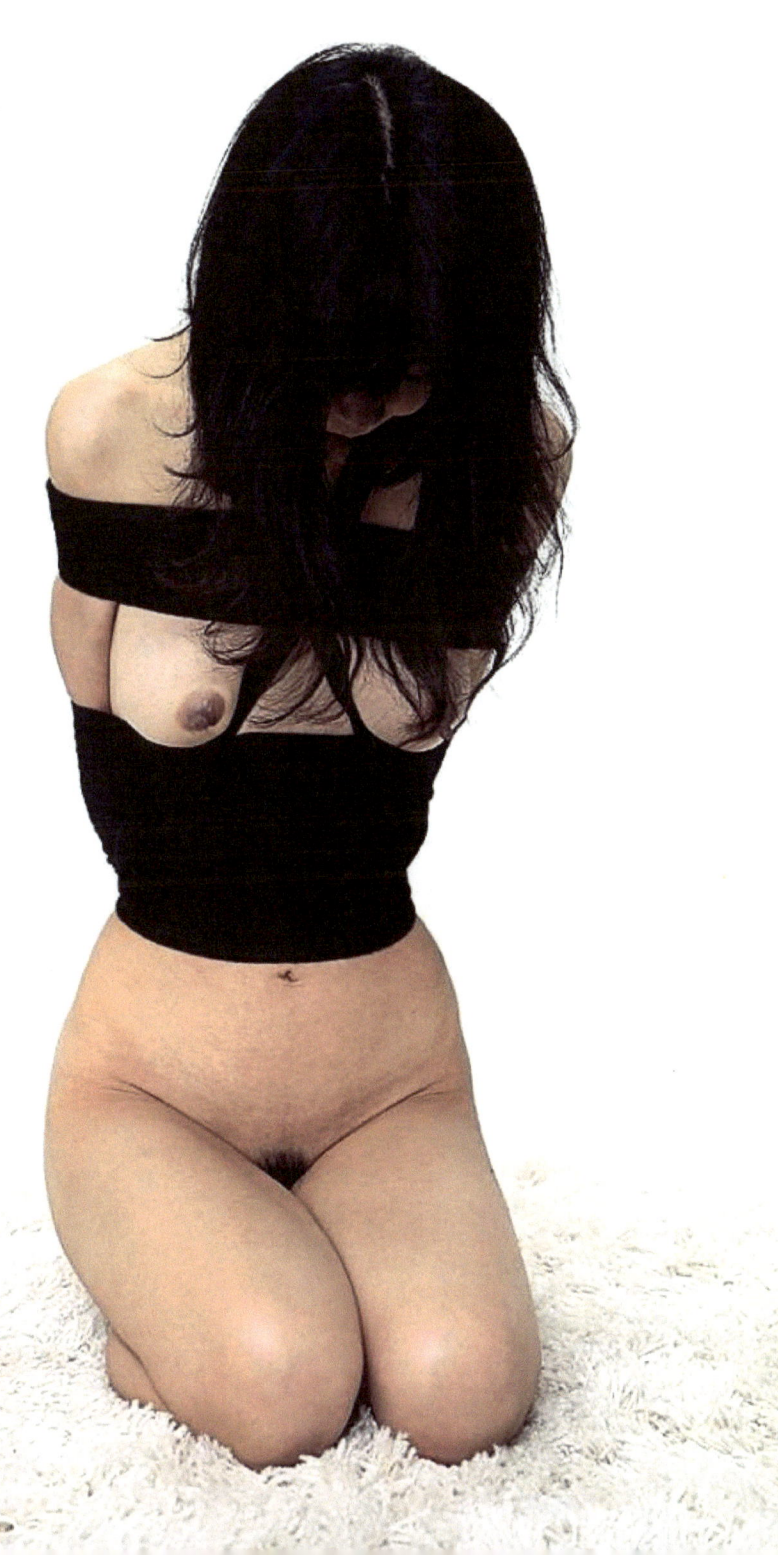

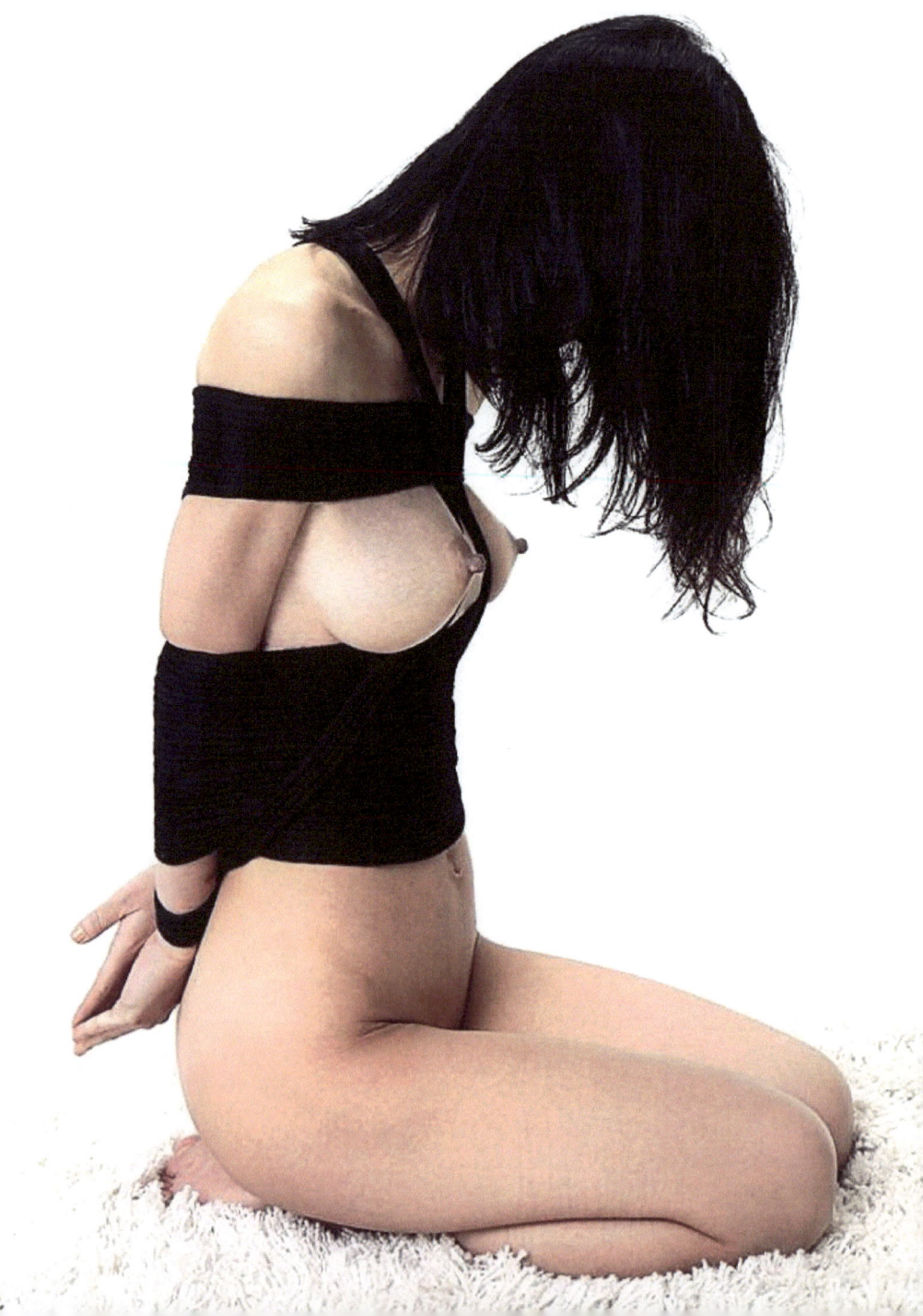

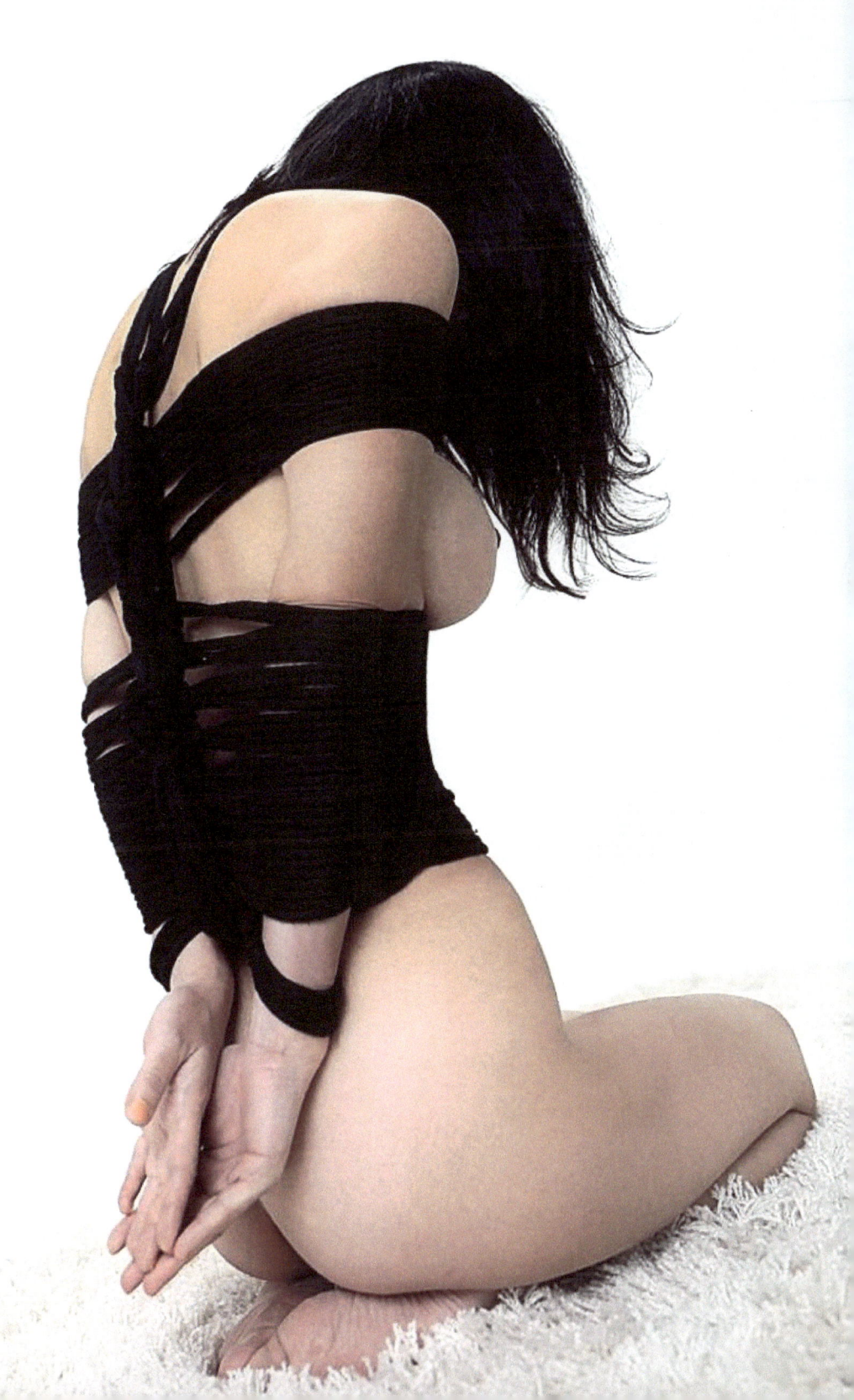

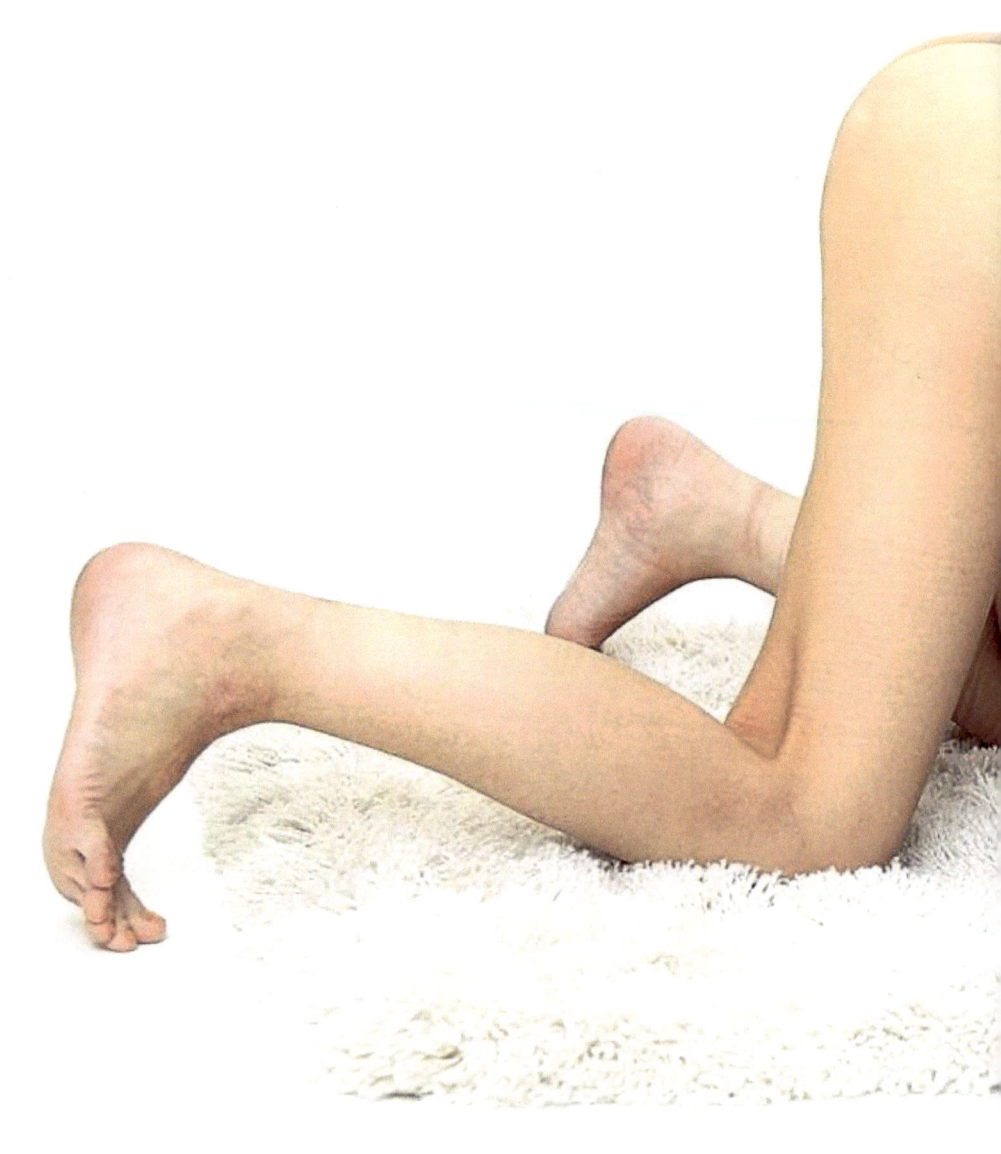

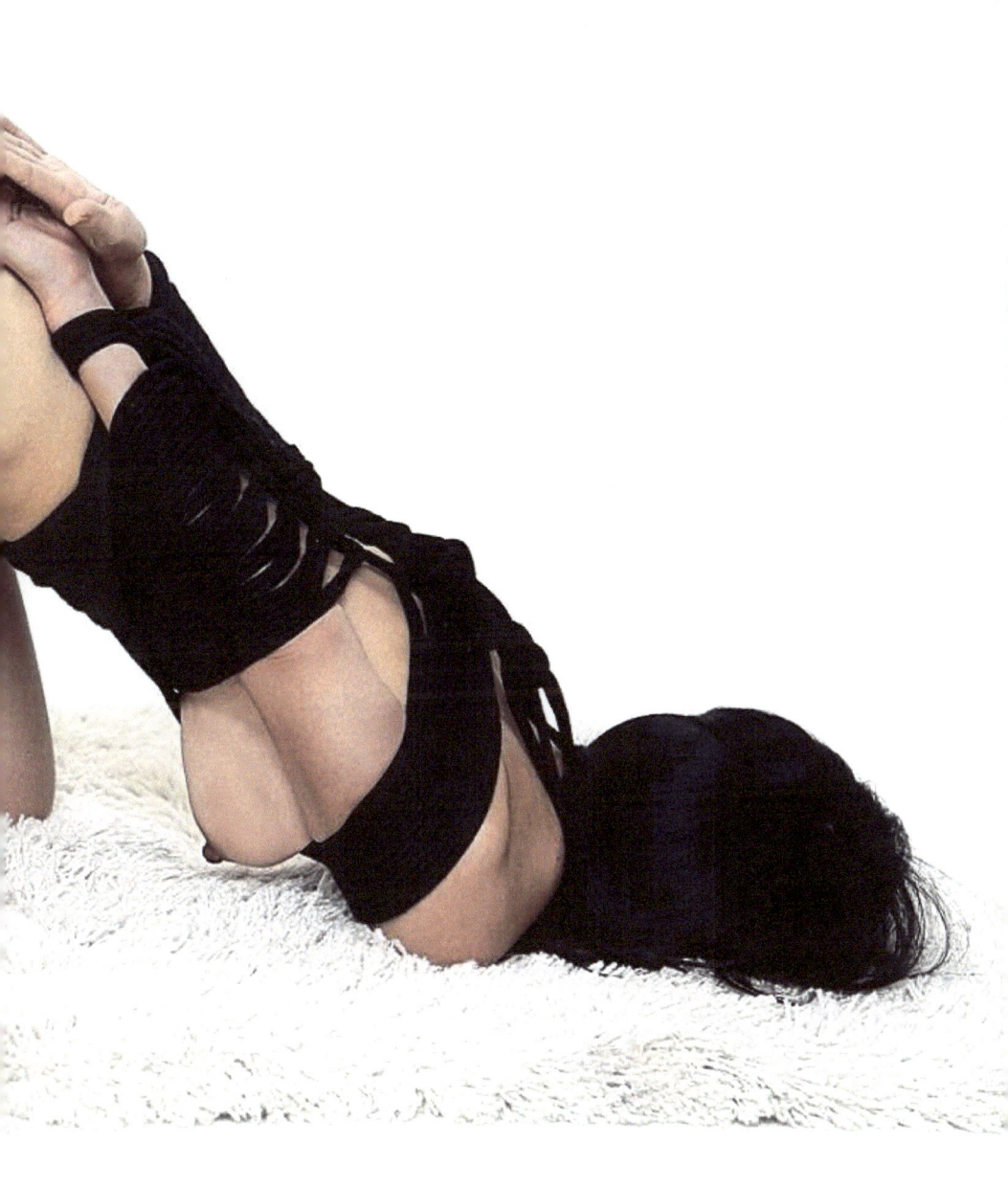

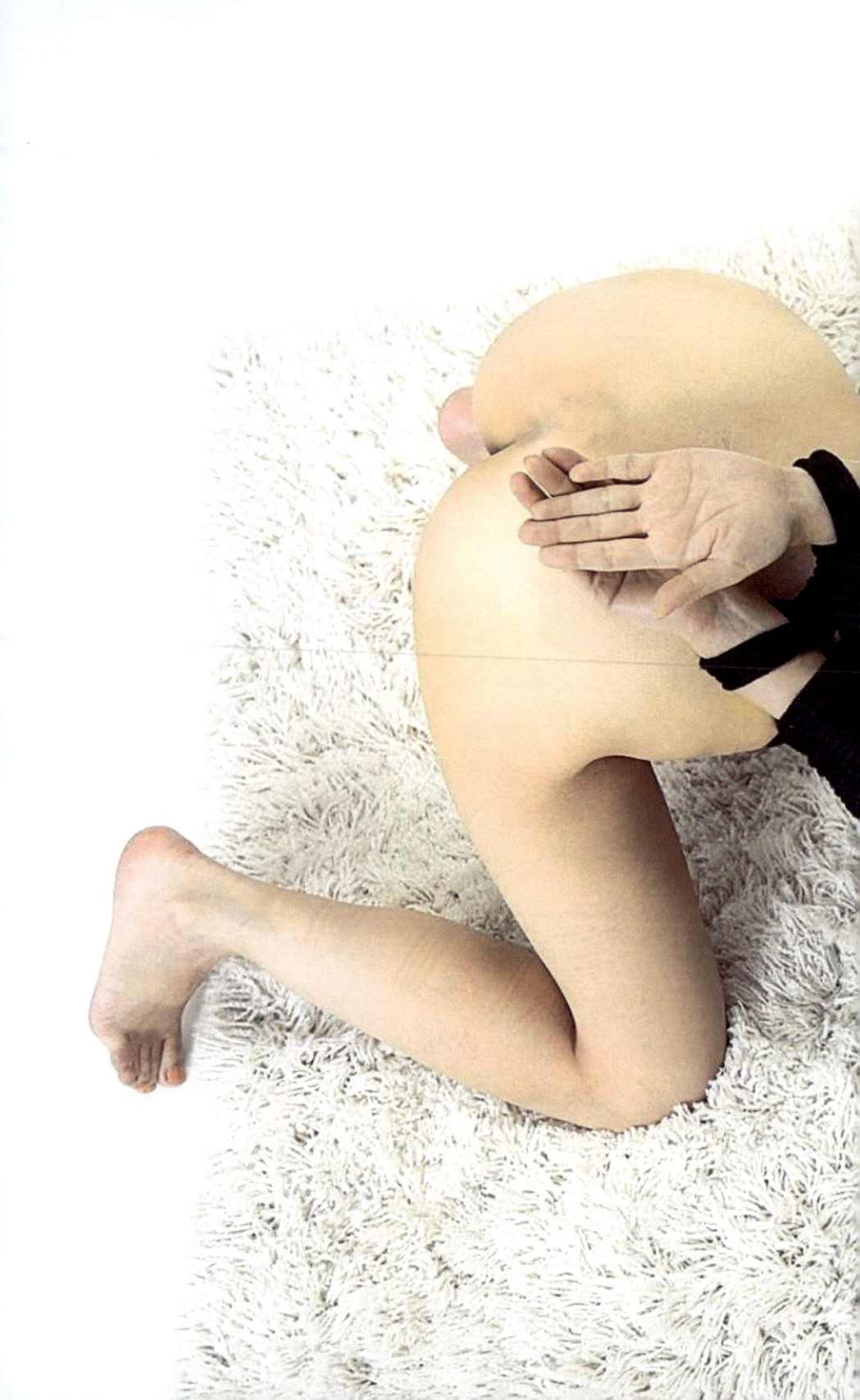

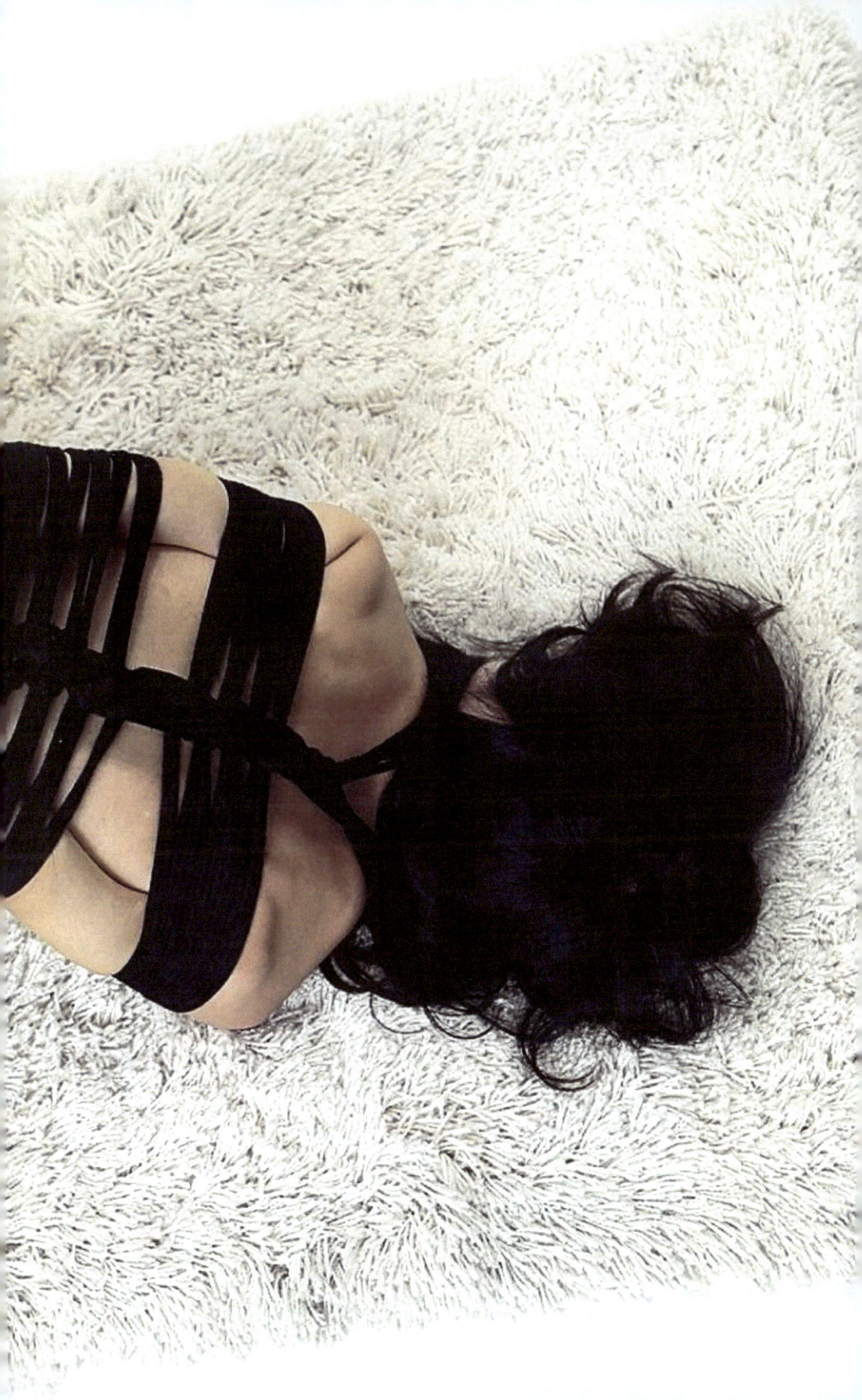

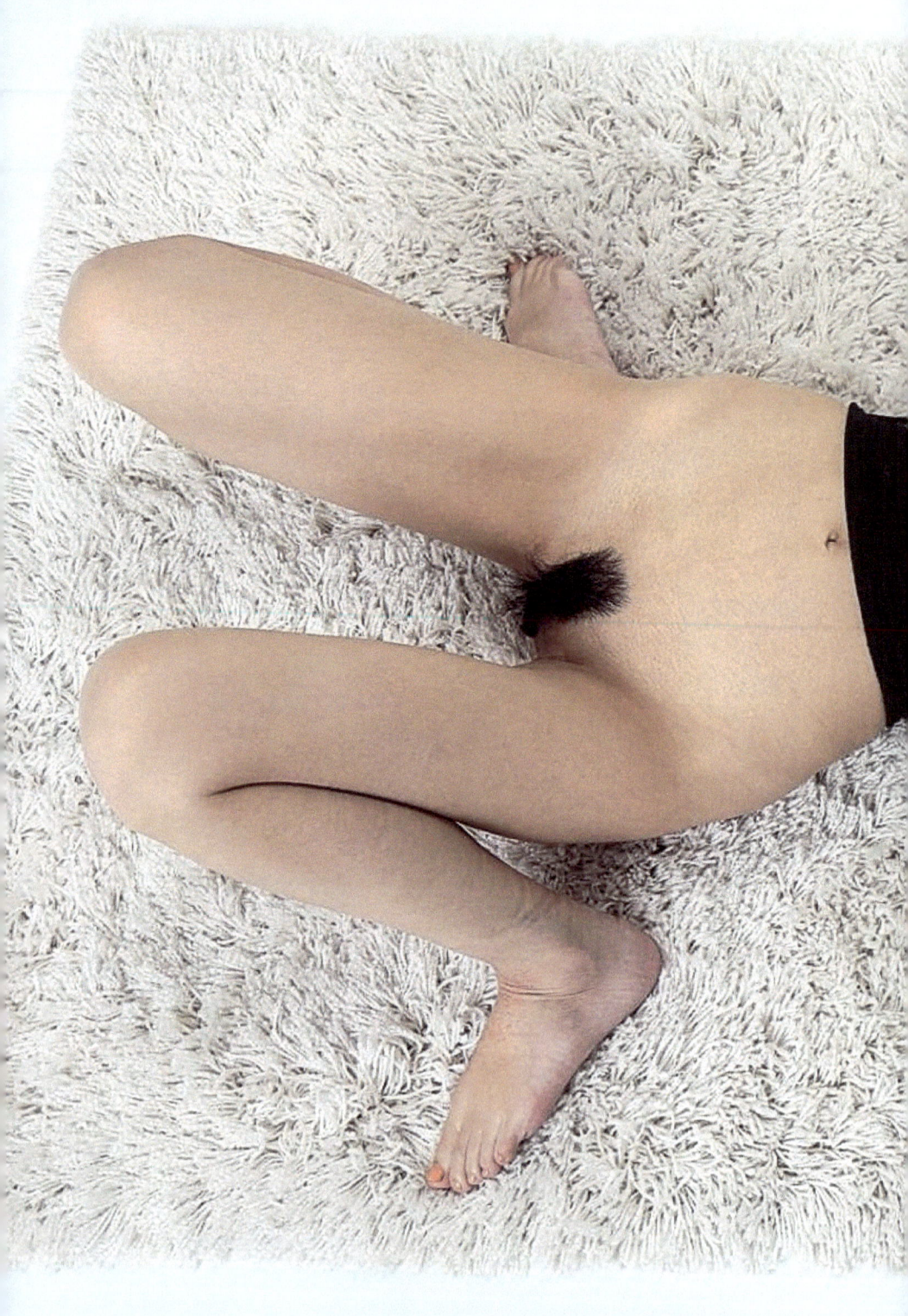

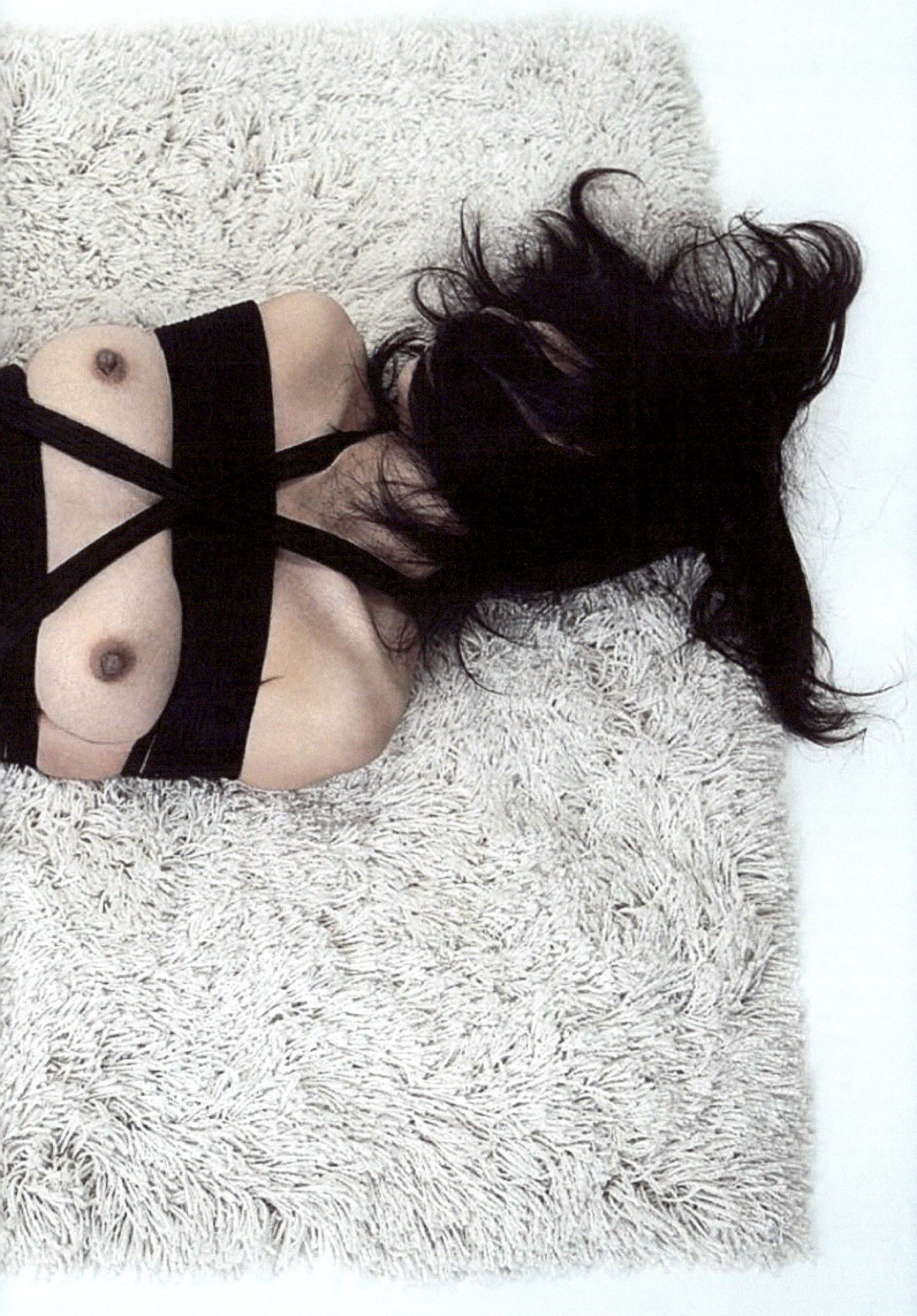

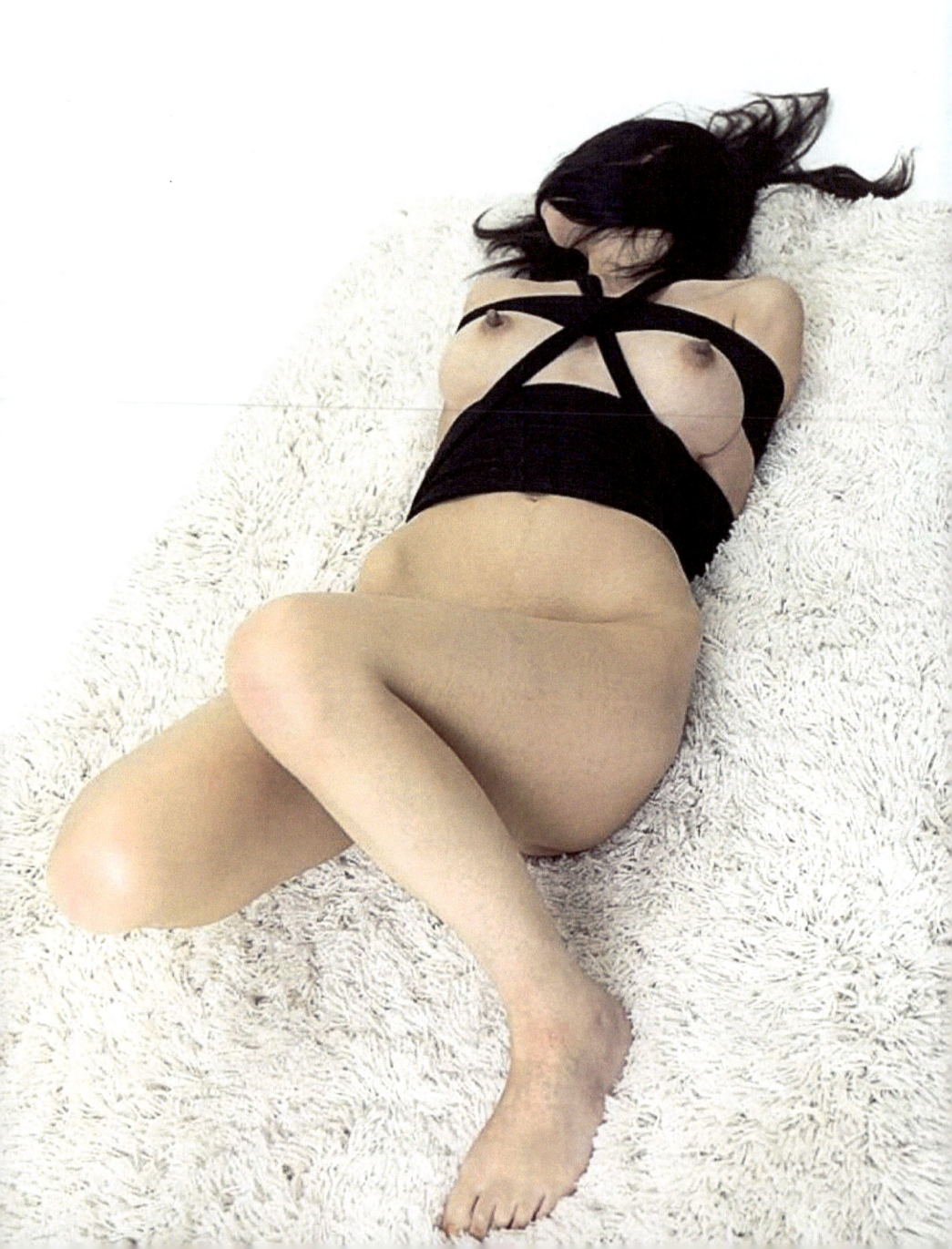

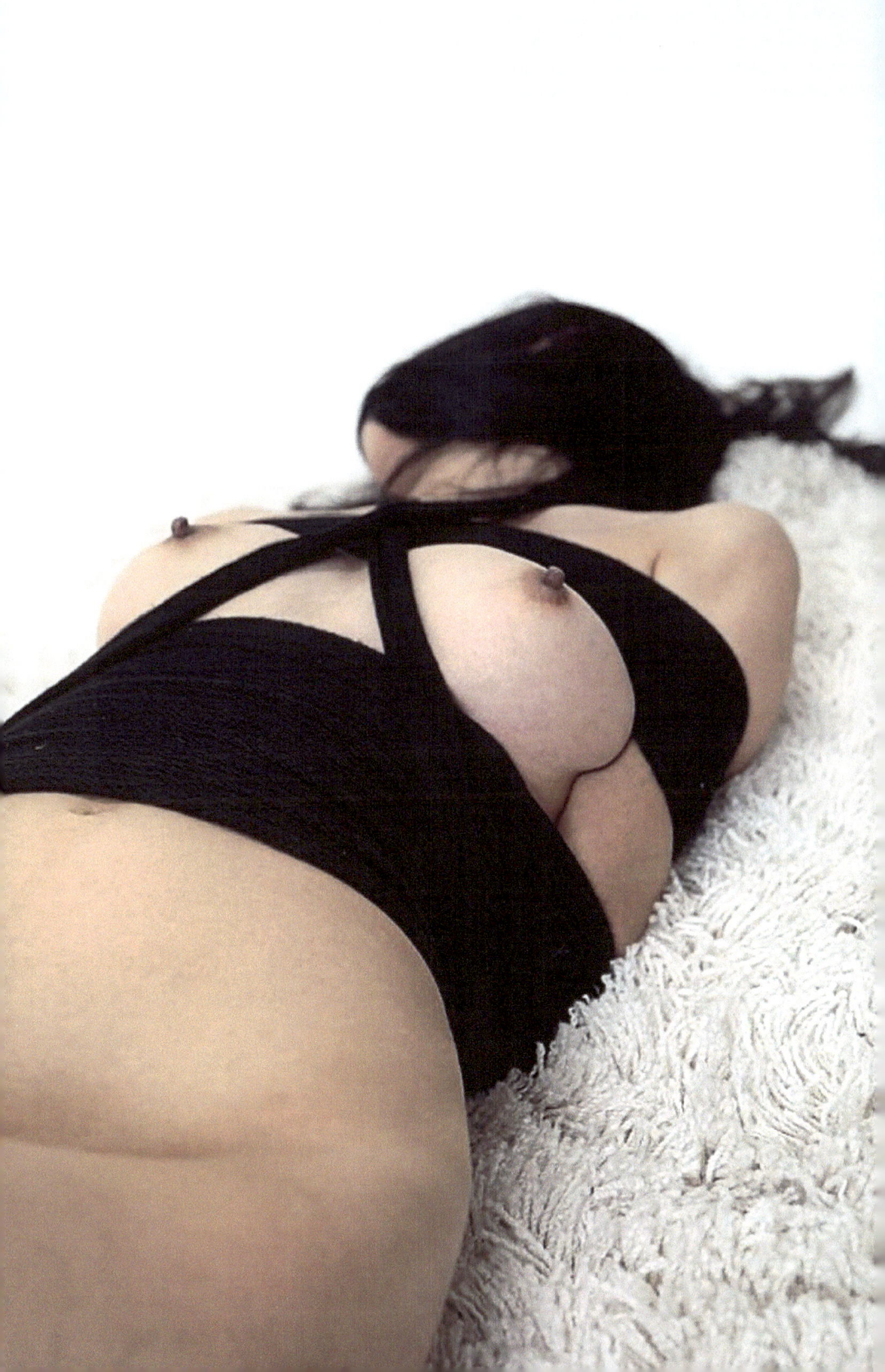

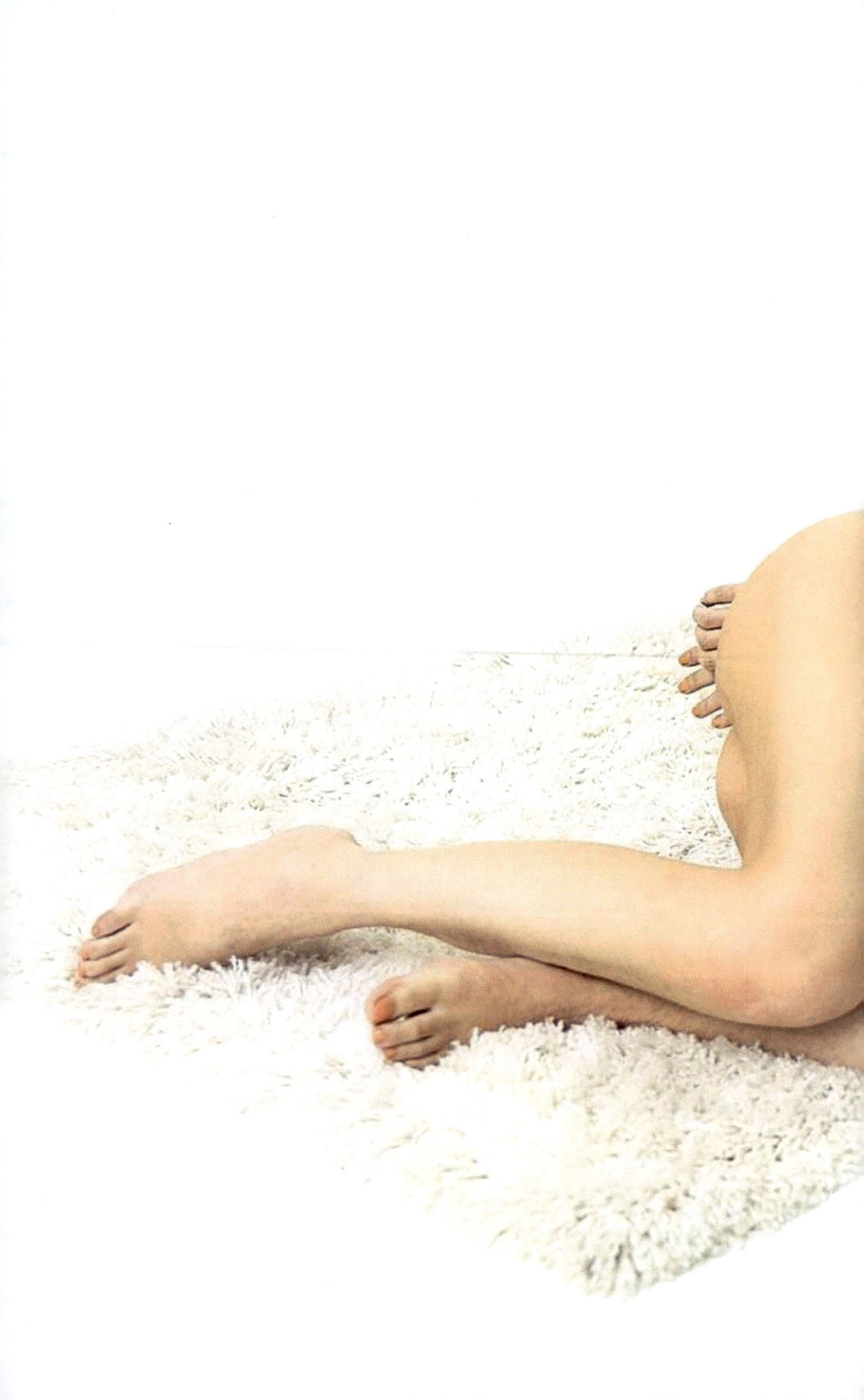

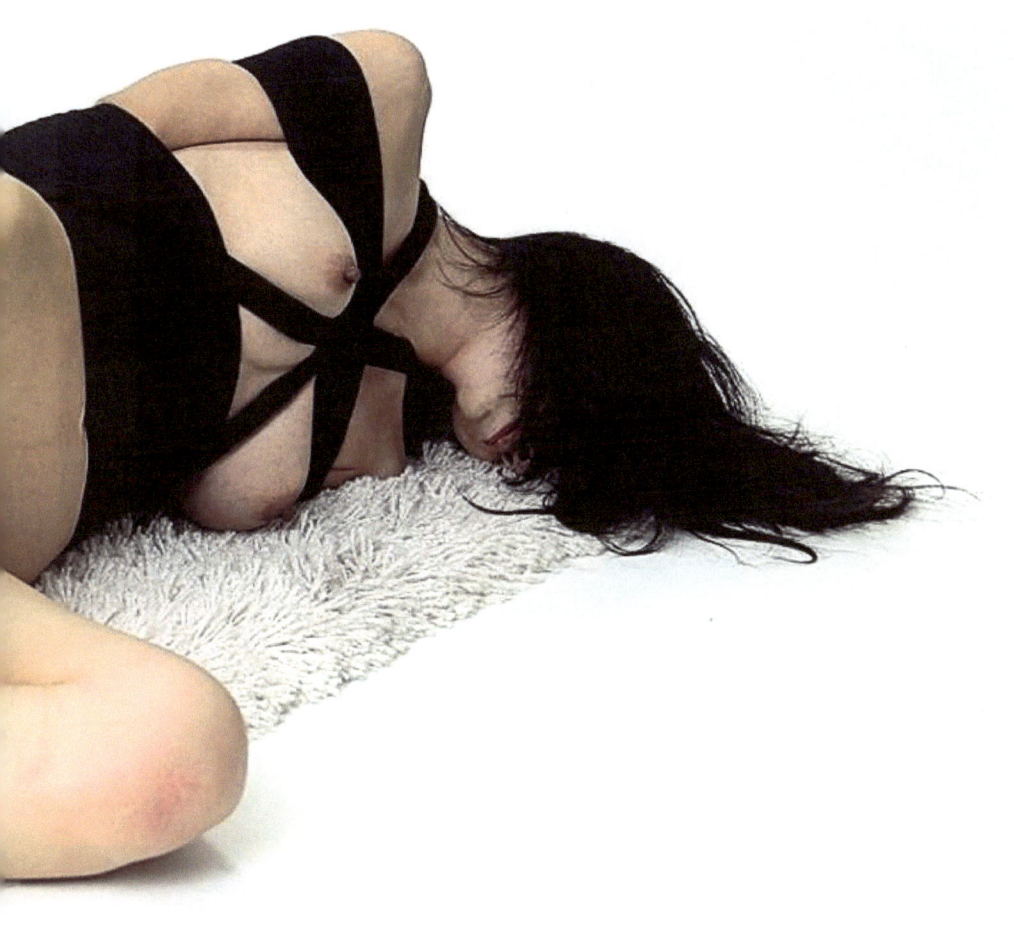

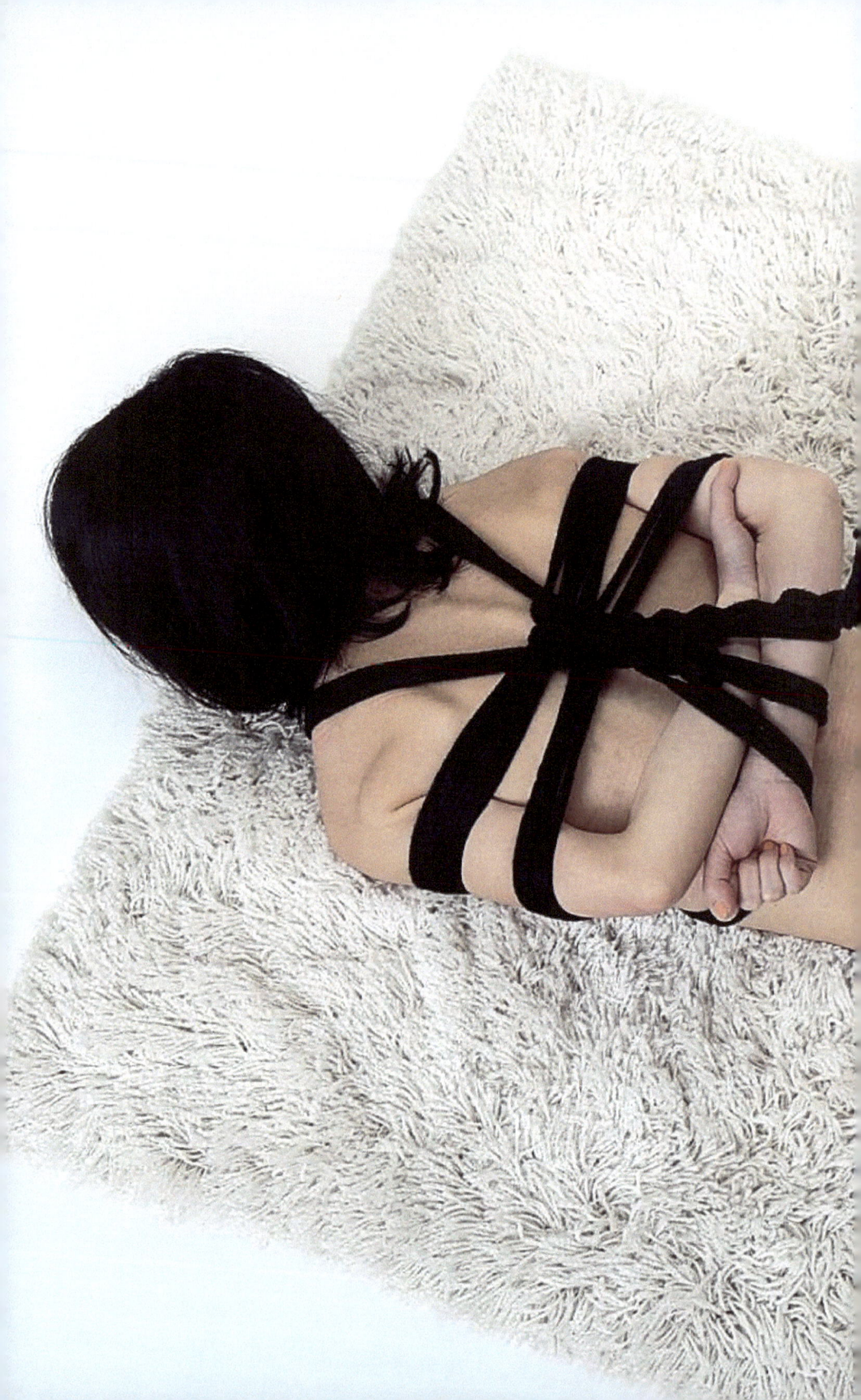

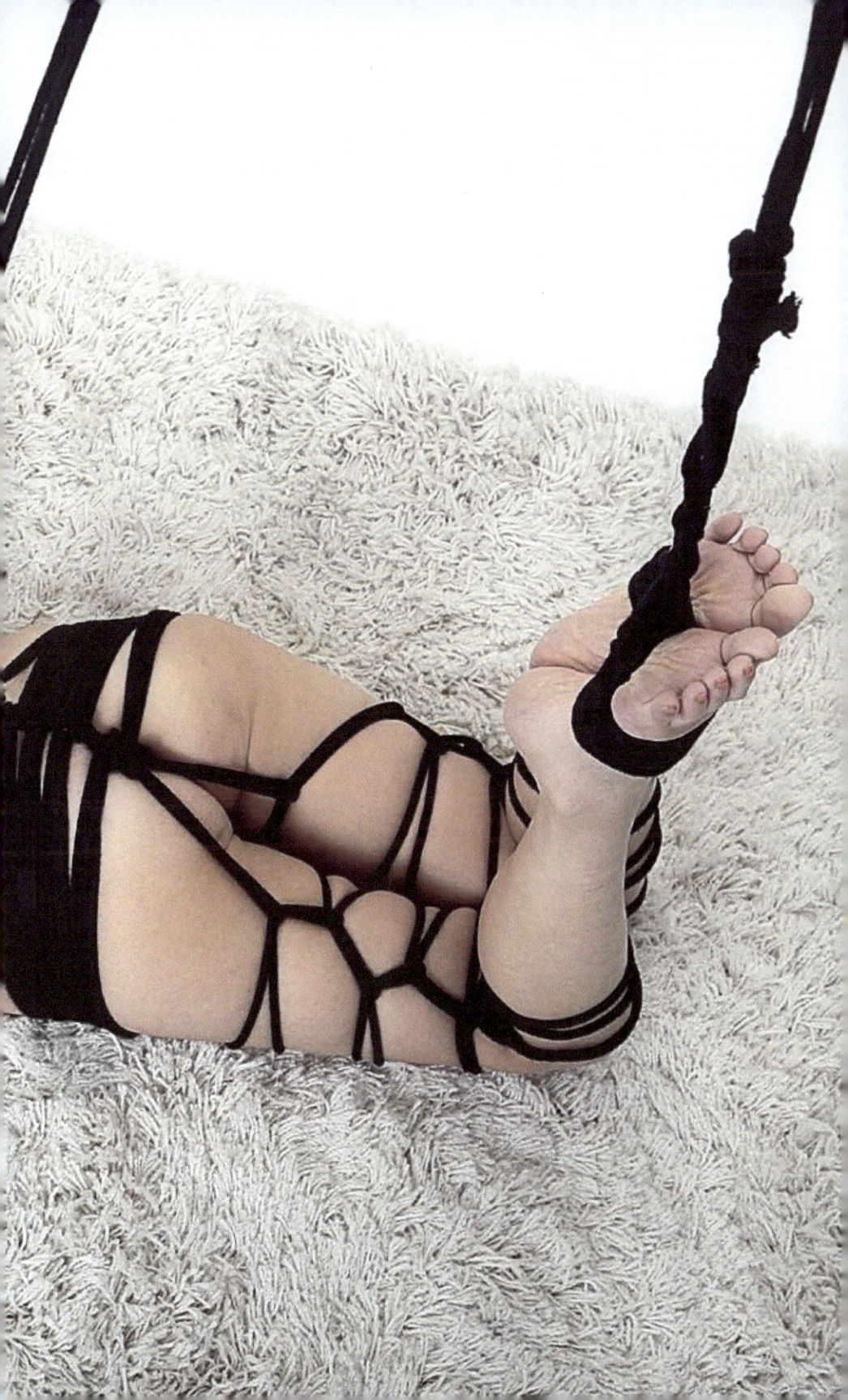

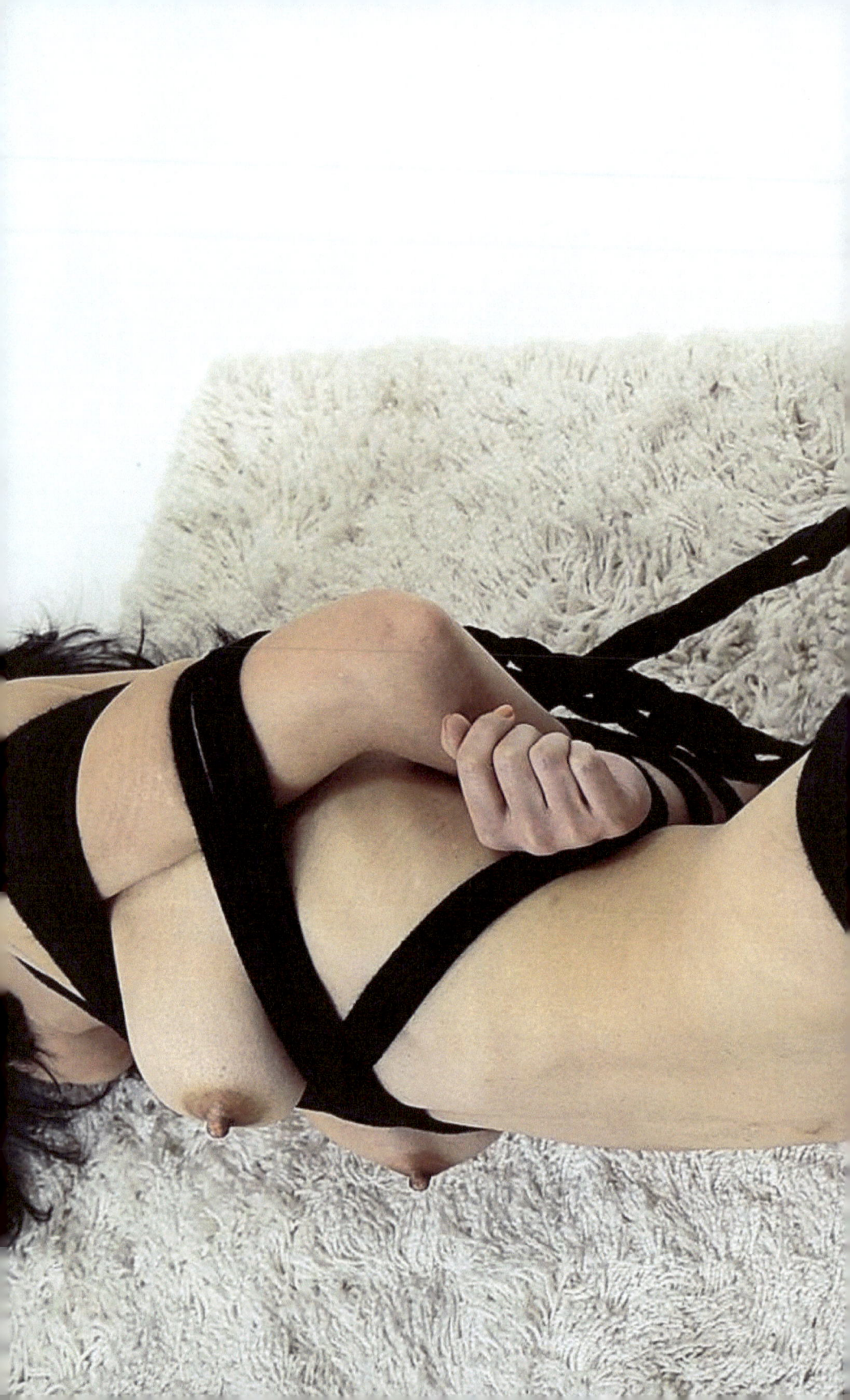

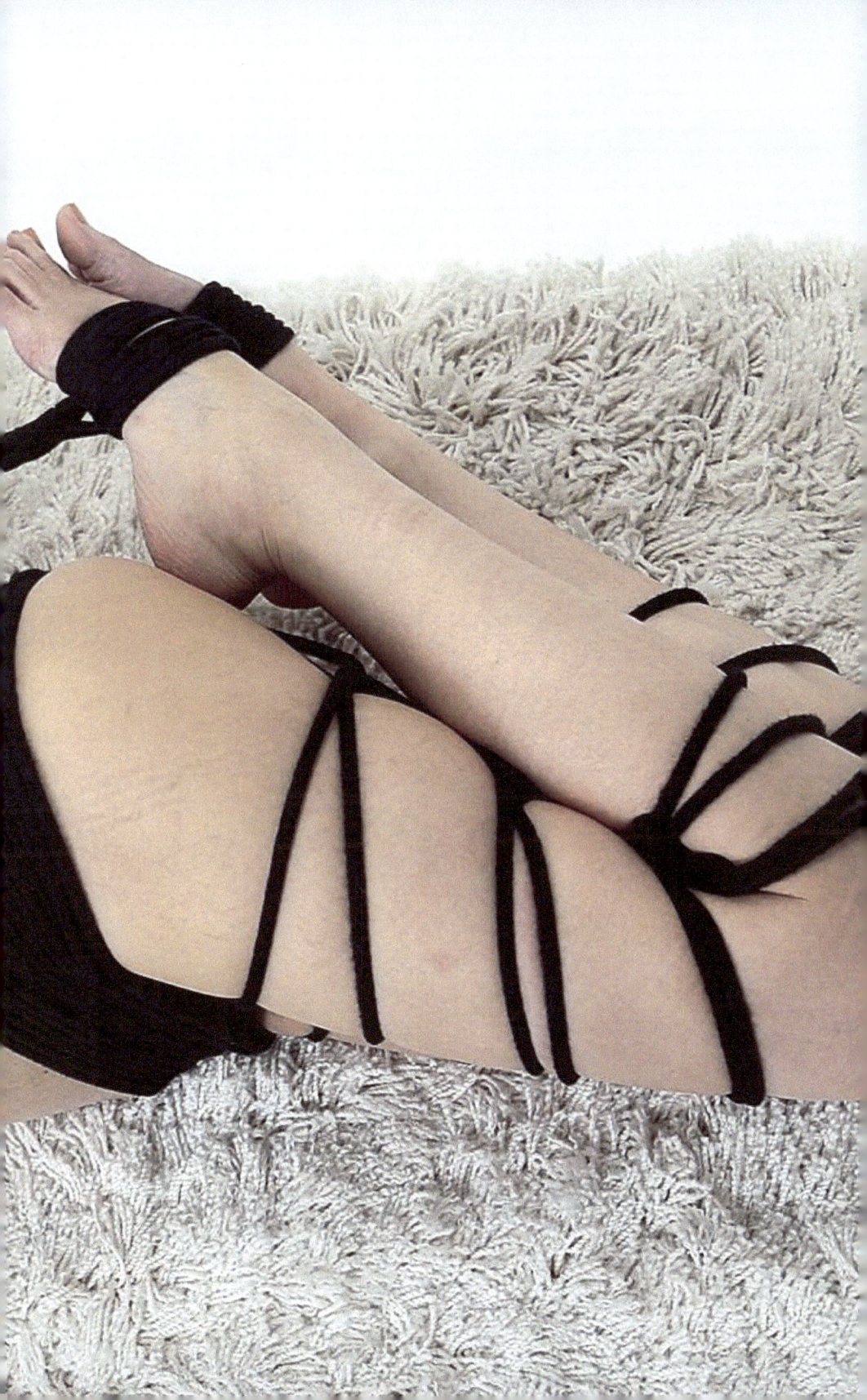

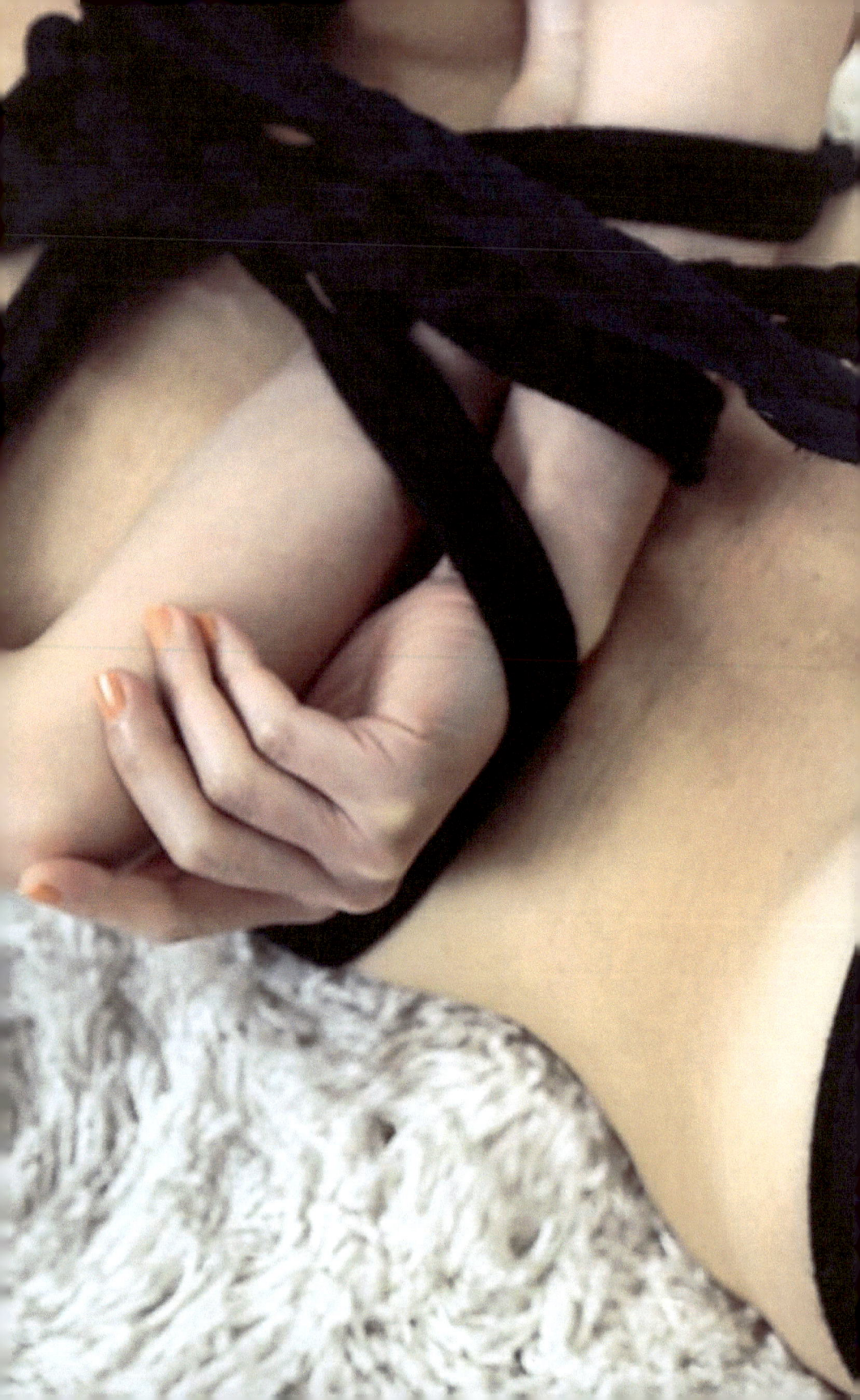

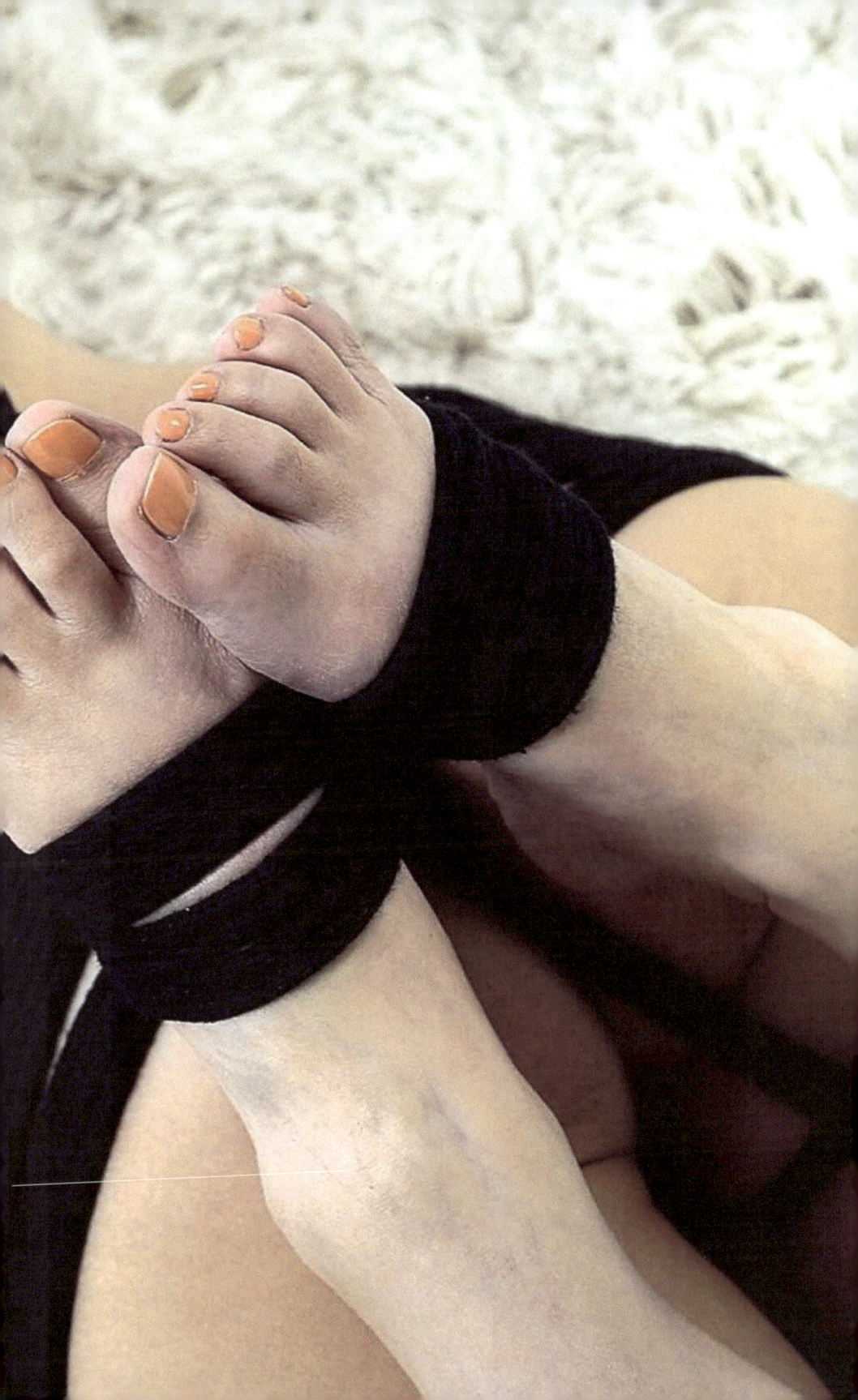

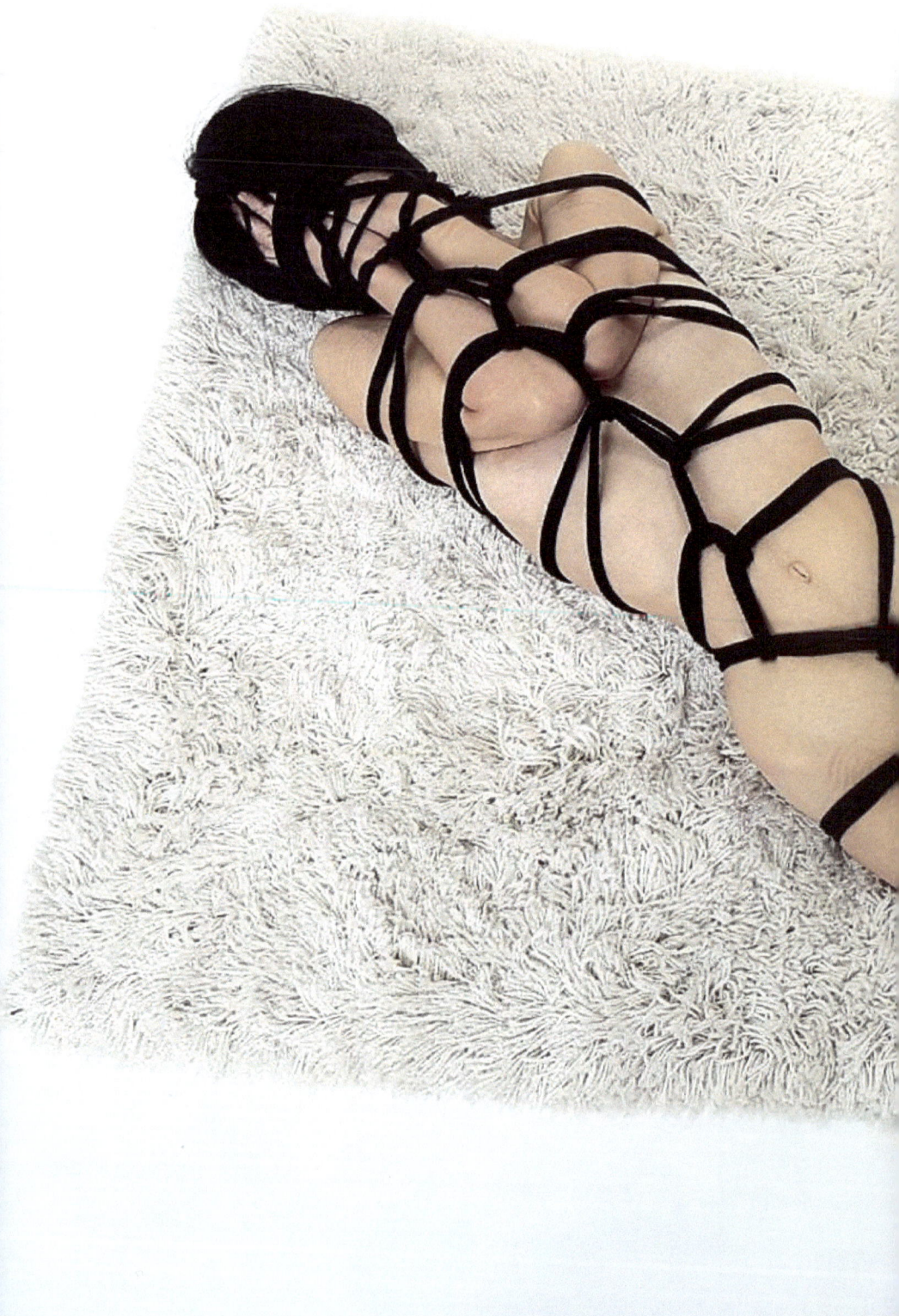

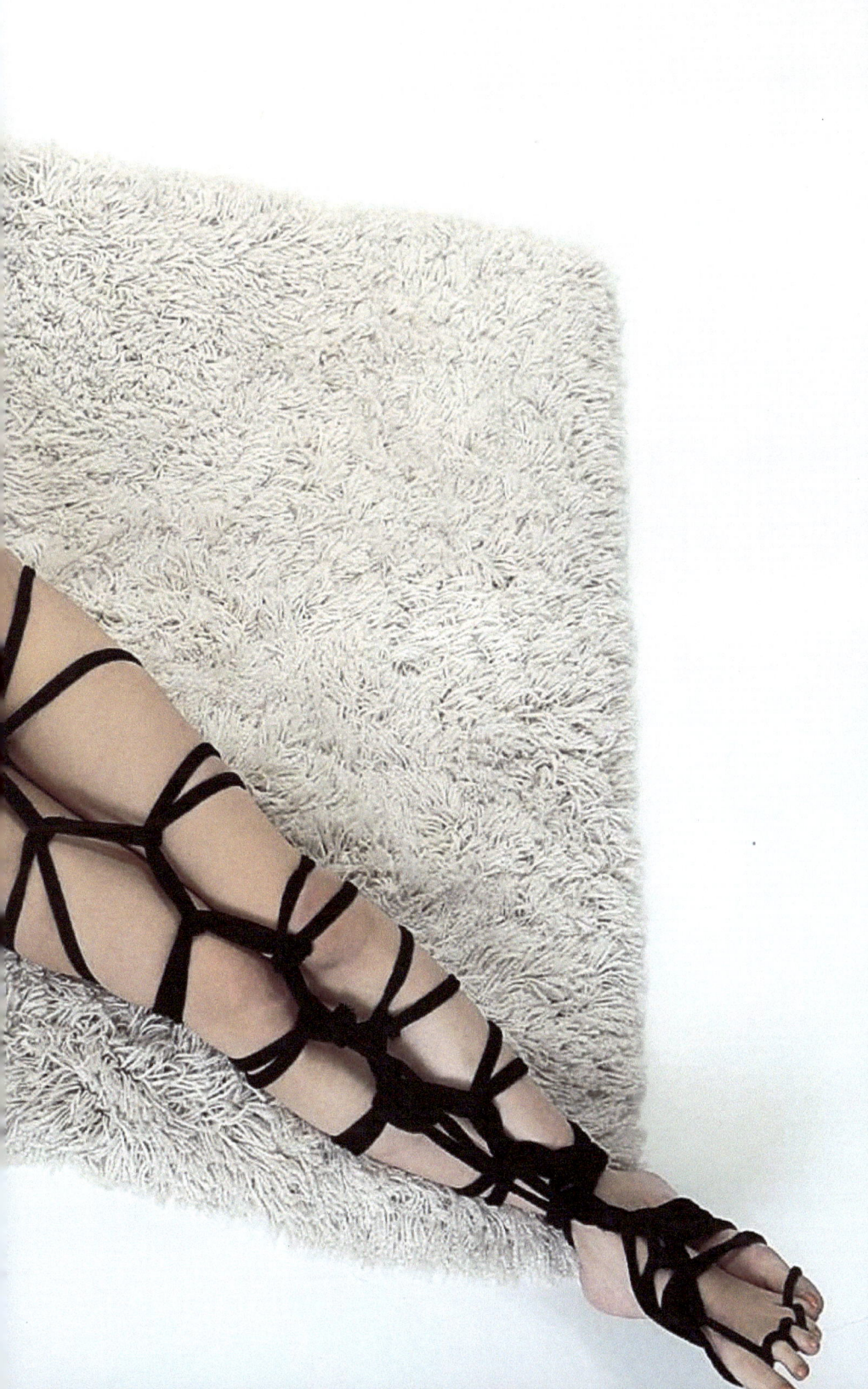

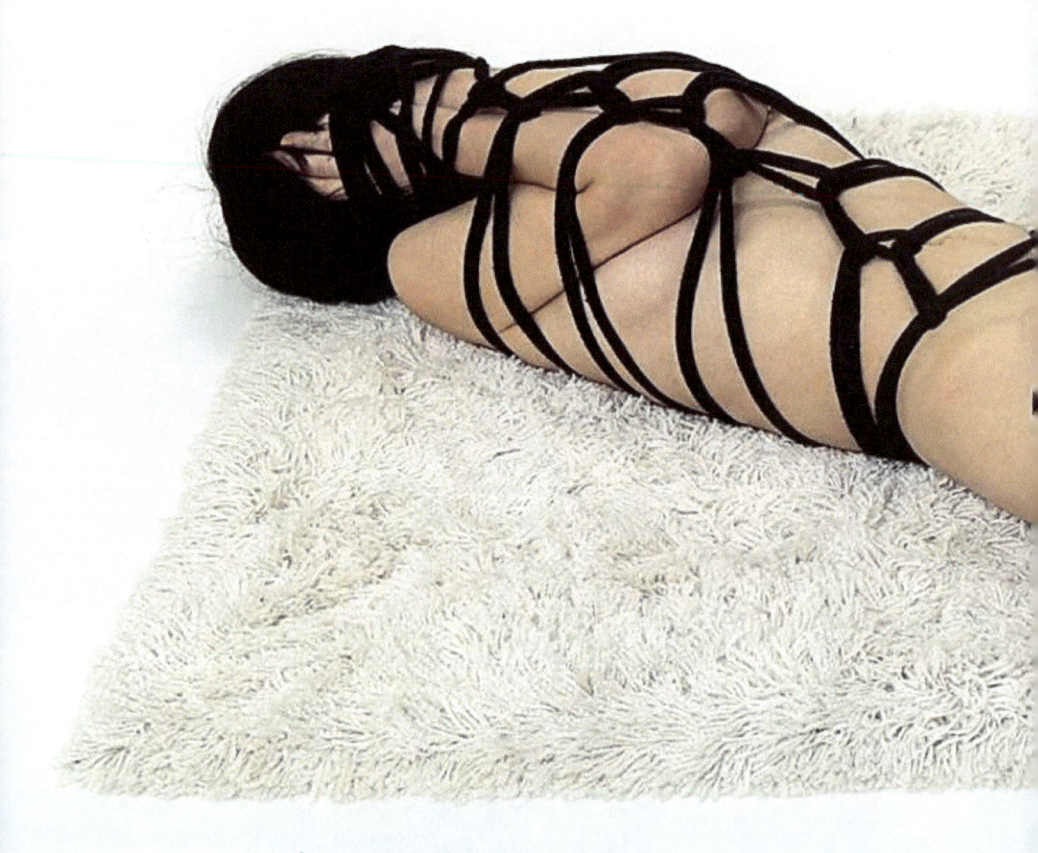

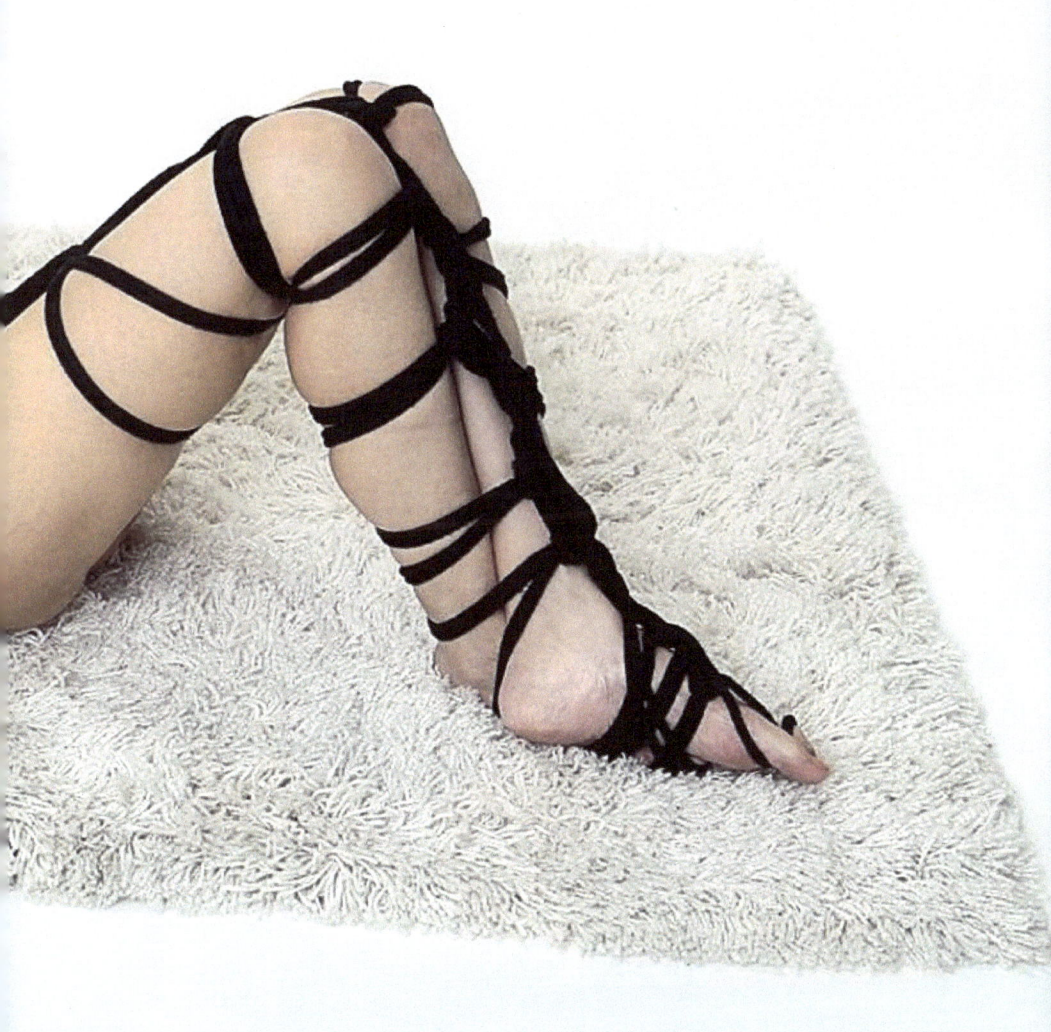

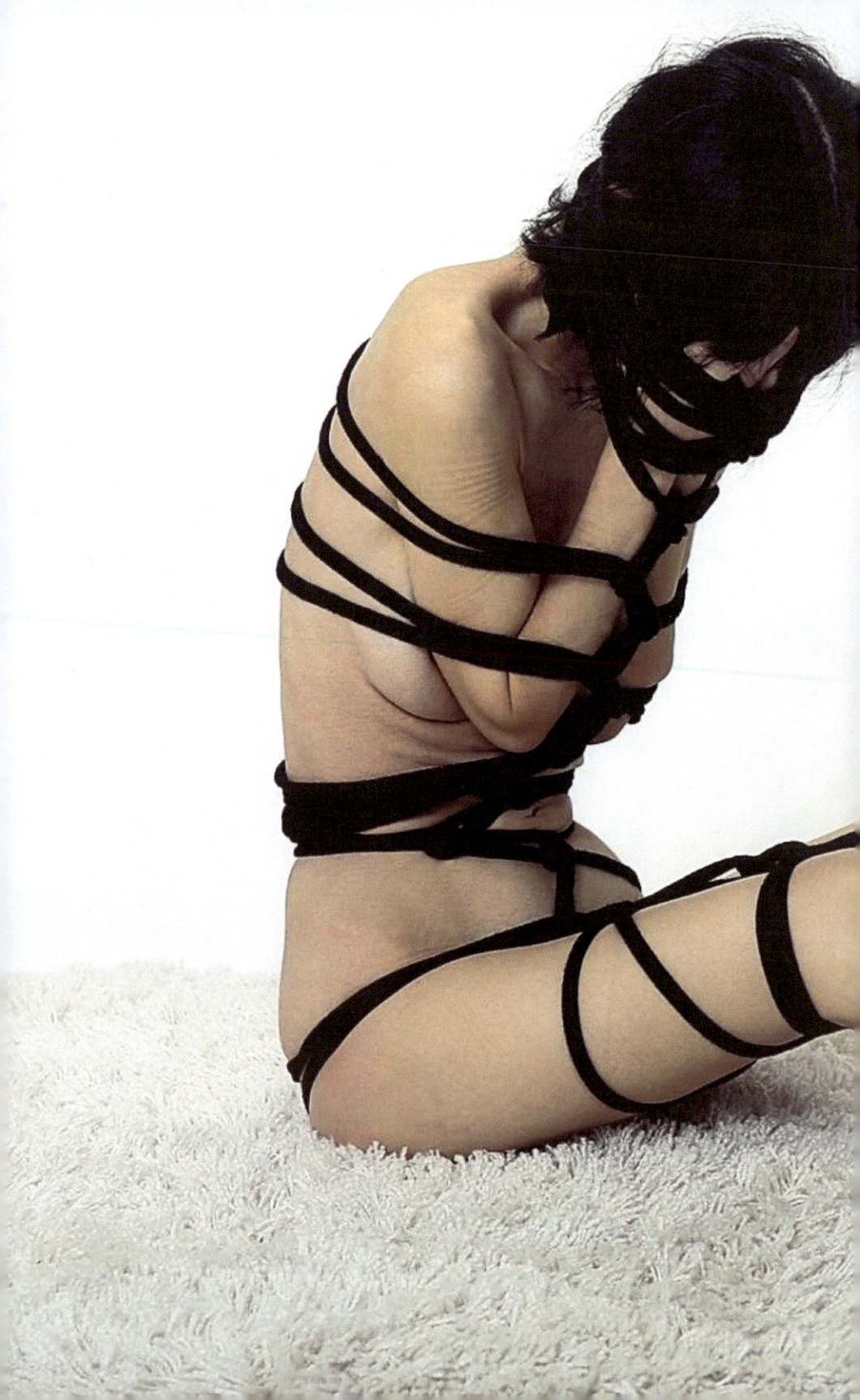

Achromatic Domination

— KINBAKU photo book —

Model: Yuki Sakurai

Rope and photo: †SIVA†

Published by: Sakura Publishing
http://sakurasm.com/English/

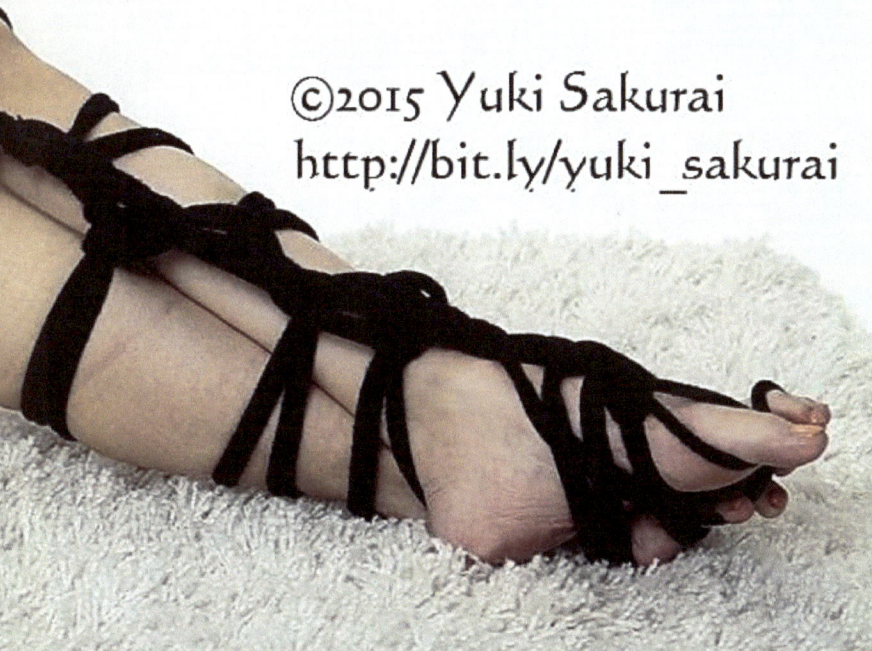